GROWING TO A RIPE OLD AGE

50 YEARS IN THE GARDEN

Summersdale Publishers Ltd
46 West Street
Chichester
West Sussex
PO19 1RP
UK

www.summersdale.com

Printed and bound by CPI Group (UK) Ltd, Croydon, CR0 4YY

ISBN: 978-1-84953-170-2

Substantial discounts on bulk quantities of Summersdale books are available to corporations, professional associations and other organisations. For details telephone Summersdale Publishers on (+44-1243-771107), fax (+44-1243-786300) or email (nicky@summersdale.com).

Edward Enfield

GROWING TO A RIPE OLD AGE

50 YEARS IN THE GARDEN

summersdale

Contents

Preface

When I finished writing this book and read it through, I realized that it gives the impression that my wife plays no part in the garden, which is not true. The rough division between us is that things inside the house are her affair, and those outside are mine, but as I am not above lending a hand with the dishes, so she has made a speciality of deadheading and bonfires, with occasional bursts of weeding. She deadheads the prickliest of roses with fearless determination, and when it comes to bonfires she is in a class of her own. She advances upon a pile of potato haulm or a heap of rose prunings equipped only with a couple of bags and a box of matches, and in no time at all the whole lot has gone up in flames. I don't know how it is done, but the chickens love it. The bonfire patch is in the chicken run, and once the fire gets going they crowd round like a lot of Hindu widows about to hurl themselves onto their husbands' funeral pyres. As soon as it dies down they take a dust bath in the ashes, somehow picking the moment when they can plunge in without singeing their feathers or actually committing suttee.

I am very grateful that she has taken these jobs off my shoulders, as, I expect, are the chickens.

House and Garden:
The Flower Show,
the Fence and the
Water Supply

I have only ever had to do with one garden, but my dealings with it have extended over fifty years, because we have lived in the same house for half a century, and the garden came with the house. It is a big garden, or so it seems to me, being about three-quarters of an acre in all. I came to it knowing nothing about growing anything, and this book is the result of the successes and failures, inventions and frustrations, discoveries and developments which were incidental to getting it to its present state. This state I regard as pretty satisfactory but by no means perfect, but then few gardens are.

Gardens, in my view, often involve too much gardening. This is partly to do with the nature of human beings, who will make a competition out of anything if they possibly can. Gardening is supposed to be like fishing, the contemplative man's recreation, but it often isn't. Just as fishermen, instead of quietly fishing, go in for competitions to see who can haul the most, or the biggest, fishes out of their natural element in a given time, so gardeners go in for flower shows with a view to smashing the opposition in the matter of growing flowers or vegetables. This can quite go to their heads, and I have known normally modest and retiring people become openly boastful from having taken first prize with a handful of French beans.

Also, there are some who open their gardens to the public. This involves them in furious labour over a short time to get every weed out, every blade of grass mown, every inch of hedge clipped, and a stake in place to support every bloom that needs it, all in order to be ready for the day of opening. They always do this for a worthy cause, often the British Red Cross, but their reward comes from basking in the admiration which every visitor feels obliged to express at the glorious state of the garden in question.

Ours is not a garden to open to the public but when it comes to flower shows, I have been through all that. In my case it was a matter of roses. Roses can become an obsession, a mania, a disease, and I caught it. There is a special society devoted to roses called the Royal National Rose Society, and I joined it. Some of the madder members refer to themselves by the fairly frightful sobriquet of 'rosarians', and while I never went as far as that, I went pretty far. I got all the society's books and used to sit up late into the night with catalogues of roses, planning and re-planning beds of different shapes with roses of different combinations to go in different parts of the garden. In my time I have grown hybrid teas, floribundas, China roses, David Austin roses, old roses, shrub roses, climbers, ramblers, and I have even tried growing roses from seed. I am pleased to say that sanity has returned and we are now down to one excellent rose bed with a few other roses here and there, and I will give my conclusions on rose growing in the proper place.

In the time of my rose mania, the flower show was the big event of the year. In the days leading up to it I sprayed vigorously against black spot and mildew, searched anxiously for signs of rust and squirted evil poison on any greenfly that showed up. I stripped all but one bud from the leading shoots in the hope of getting one perfect bloom on each. When I cut them for the show, I pulled off any nasty-looking petals and stripped away any unsightly leaves. If there was any sign of mildew on the remaining leaves I wiped them with methylated spirits, which is a trick supposed to fool the judges. Then I went early to the show tent and put them in the proper place, and hurried back as soon as the show opened to see how I had got on. I had my ups and downs, but I am pleased to say that I was sometimes rewarded with a red sticker saying 'First' and a prize of ten shillings.

Because of this I got a bit of a reputation as a man who knew a thing or two about roses, so people used sometimes to consult me about problems with theirs. Thrips were what impressed them most. Not many people know about thrips, so they would show me a mottled, sick-looking bud that was obviously going to come to no good, then ask me what was wrong. 'Thrips!' I would say with an air of great wisdom, and then add, 'Look, I will show you.' Then I would peel back the outside petals and if they looked closely they could catch a glimpse of some nasty little black creatures scurrying for cover. From time to time they would show me roses that were not looking too good and if I couldn't see what was wrong with them I would say firmly, 'Weather damage!' No one ever asked me what I meant by weather damage, which was just as well, as I have no idea, I just cribbed the phrase from someone else.

I gave up the flower show business mainly because I had had enough, but partly because of one particular flower show where I felt I had rather disgraced myself. It wasn't my fault really, but the fault of some Siamese children.

People who come from Thailand are now called Thais, but in those days they were still called Siamese. We had a Siamese family staying with us, made up of two parents with three children aged perhaps fourteen, twelve and ten, and we took them to the flower show. At that time our local show was a pretty big affair, with all sorts of stalls and entertainments on the side, one of which was a bottle stall, i.e. a stall of bottles which could be won by throwing a small rubber ring cleanly over the neck of any particular bottle. I now believe that Siamese children of those times must have spent many hours in the nursery throwing rubber rings over the necks of bottles, because they were extraordinarily adept at it. Every so often, while we were in the marquee looking at the flowers, a Siamese boy would rush up and press a bottle of wine upon one of us, and then rush off, to be back soon after with a bottle of gin. It all got out of hand and they had to be warned off and barred from further competition.

As if that were not enough, the girl of the party wandered over to where there was a game of skittles going on. She paid her entry fee, picked up the ball, and at first go knocked over all the skittles. They put them up again, so she knocked them over again. The family name was Chakrabandhu, and the announcer had some difficulty with it when asking for Miss Chakrabandhu to come and collect her cash, she having won both the ladies' and the open bowling competitions. I think her prizes came to serious money, such as £7 for the ladies' prize and £10 for the open, and while nobody actually said anything, I felt they eyed me askance for having arrived with these slightly swarthy young assassins who ruthlessly plundered the show. This in itself was not enough to end my showing career, but it tipped the scales. I was getting tired of it anyway, and thought I had better leave off.

But now, before I come to the garden as it is, I should describe the garden as it was when we acquired it. We bought the house from an elderly couple of whom the lady said to us on first acquaintance: 'I used to be a dent.' This was a puzzling remark, until we realized that her maiden name had been Dent, and that she came from the family of Dent the publishers. Either from old age, or lack of interest, or lack of time, they had let the garden get into a pretty poor state. There was a rough lawn with some awkwardly placed and overgrown flower beds, a rose bed with some old decrepit roses, and a meaningless archway which led nowhere but was covered with honeysuckle. Otherwise it was largely jungle.

Along one side, between us and the field next door, there was an inadequate fence. Its purpose was to keep the farmer's livestock out of our garden, at which it conspicuously failed. I had the idea, perhaps from something in the title deeds, that it was my responsibility to keep this fence in good repair, but in those days we were short of money, so I could not then do what I would do now, and find a man who does fencing and say to him 'Fence!' whereupon he would fence it. It is a long fence, of some 100 yards, and I spent a lot of time with a hammer and staples and a spade and posts and wire trying to make it impregnable, but there was something about our side of it which our neighbour's livestock found irresistible. We have come home on a wet afternoon to find the garden full of cows, and I remember telephoning my neighbour at two in the morning to ask him to take his horse off our lawn. There are a few deer around in this part of Sussex, and they simply regarded this fence as a rather feeble challenge which they used to hop over to graze on the shoots of the roses or, when I started to grow strawberries, to eat the plants. The final solution to the fencing problem only came about when my neighbour decided to erect new fences in all his fields at one go and included this fence in the operation. Since then there have been no cows or deer in the garden. Deer could jump it if they put their minds to it, but they don't, possibly because there is now a greyhound on our side, which may put them off the idea.

As well as the fence problem, there was a water problem, though this mainly affected the house and had only a marginal impact on the garden. There was no mains water, only a well, and while there was nothing wrong with the well there was a great deal wrong with the pump. You may find my description incomprehensible, but the water was supposed to be lifted from the well to a tank in the roof by one of those pumps which has an upright handle which you push and pull backwards and forwards by hand. That, at least, is what normal people do, but in our case there was an arrangement that can only have been devised by a lunatic. The pump was in a lean-to outhouse, and the lunatic in question had tried to mechanize the whole thing with an electric motor and an upside-down bicycle.

The electric motor was connected to the back wheel of the upside-down bicycle by a thin leather belt. When you switched it on, the motor turned a small wheel which turned the belt which turned the bicycle wheel, which caused the pedals to go round. One pedal was connected to the pump handle by a complicated set of shafts, and the effect of the pedal going round was to send the main shaft into a seemingly circular motion which somehow wagged the pump handle to and fro and so pumped the water. The whole thing looked like a Heath Robinson joke, and if it had worked it would have been a good joke, but as it didn't, it was a very bad one.

The entire device suffered from all ills to which both pumps and bicycles are prone. To do it justice, the electric motor never failed, but the leather belt used to slip off, stretch or break, and have to be taken to the cobbler to be mended. The chain used to come off the bicycle, and the pedal off the shaft. When it was working the pump seemed to lift about an eggcupful of water at every stroke, so that it had to run for hours on end and the tank never got full. As we had a seven-month-old baby when we moved in, this chronic water shortage was a serious matter.

Of course any sensible person would have scrapped the whole thing and bought a proper electric pump. However, we were, as I mentioned, short of money, and furthermore before we had reached the point of deciding that the whole thing was hopeless, the good news came that the water board was going to lay a main near our house, and we could, if we wished, be connected to it. Naturally we did wish, and naturally it took some time for this to happen, what with the digging of trenches and laying of pipes and filling in of forms and signing of agreements. To speed things along as much as possible, every time anyone asked me to sign anything, I signed it at once, and if they asked for money, I gave it immediately. My neighbour, though, being a man of a rather belligerent disposition, managed to get into a dispute with the water board about their charges for connecting us, so for some tantalising days the water was there, in front of our house, but we could not have it. Everything that needed to be done in the plumbing line had been done, but the water board said that we and the main could not be joined together until our neighbour cooled off and climbed down. This he did eventually, and it was a fine moment when we turned a tap and got a great rush of water, after which the electric motor, bicycle and pump became nothing more than a memory, and for the first time I could water the garden with a hose.

The soil of our garden I can best describe as unforgiving clay. Sussex clay is good for growing grass and trees and roses, but it is tricky stuff to cultivate. Its favourite winter state is that of a sort of sticky porridge, with which you can do nothing, and from this it passes rapidly to its summer state of semi concrete, with which you can do very little. There are a few days when it is changing from one state to the other, and you have to watch out and catch it on one of those days if you want to go in for any serious cultivation. I have found that it absorbs farmyard manure, compost and lime without there being any apparent change to its essential nature. I have got a way of dealing with it, however, which I will explain when I get to the matter of vegetable growing.

So much for the house and garden as they were. The garden as it is now has three parts: the part where we sit or move around, the part from which we get things to eat, and the part where the chickens enjoy a happy and peaceful life. I will deal with each in turn, starting with the sitting and moving around part, which I will call by the perhaps presumptuous and decidedly old-fashioned name of the Pleasure Garden. I only call it that for the purposes of this book, and you may be relieved to know that I do not make remarks such as 'I am going to take a nap in the Pleasure Garden', but I don't know what else to call it.

The Pleasure Garden:
Minimalism; Grass and Trees; Climbers, Pots and Advertising Copywriters

I f I could have the time again, I would start with a minimalist garden. We have a near neighbour who has a fine minimalist garden, and my sister has a semi-minimalist garden, while my daughter has a garden that is minimalist-plus; I myself never thought of anything along those lines until too late.

People with minimalist tastes live in flats or houses with almost no furniture, and my neighbour with his minimalist garden has grass and trees, but almost nothing else. He has a great sweep of lawn, which he keeps meticulously mown, and he has some very fine trees which obviously get no attention at all, except perhaps an occasional trim around the bottom of the trunks. As a departure from pure minimalism he has one round bed of day lilies, which flower in the day lily season and otherwise produce leaves. I have never noticed him giving it any attention, so perhaps it doesn't need any, which is in accordance with the principle of minimalism. He has no hedge, and so he has no hedge trimming to do. The whole is open to the road, and backed by woods behind. The general effect, as you pass, is peaceful and impressive.

My sister's semi-minimalist garden should properly be described as Darwinian, being based on the principle of the survival of the fittest. There is a large lawn and there are trees, which provide the basis of minimalism, but the previous owner left a legacy of extensive herbaceous borders. These would have demanded, if she had been prepared to give it, almost all my sister's time for relentless planting and weeding and pruning and clipping and spraying and staking and watering and all that sort of thing, so she has very wisely abandoned these borders to nature. Ground elder is the prevailing feature, with a few such things as hardy climbers and stout-hearted hollyhocks slugging it out here and there. A man comes and cuts the grass for her, and the effect is by no means bad. By applying the Darwinian principle she has saved herself the trouble and expense of digging out and grassing over the flower beds, which the strictest interpretation of minimalism would require.

My daughter has a small garden in Brighton, and I call it minimalist-plus because, while it has a couple of trees, a lawn and no flower beds, the lawn does not have to be mown as it is made of artificial plastic grass. As she has three young children who want to play in it a lot of the time, and as the artificial grass is very hard-wearing and always looks green, this is an admirable arrangement. She has flowers in pots, and it is always tidy and often colourful.

The mention of children brings me back to the matter of our own garden, which needs to be put into context. For thirty-two of the fifty years during which we have lived here, I went out to work in an office. My wife was largely, and I partly, occupied with the demands of an increasing number of children up to a total of four. There was a varying number of ponies, up to a maximum of three. There were at first a couple of whippets, and later a succession of greyhounds. A cat called Willow was succeeded by a cat called Rupert. The children wanted such things as a sandpit and a climbing frame and a paddling pool and a swing, and so you will understand that the garden had to make do with such attention as could be spared from the rest of life.

It took, nevertheless, a lot of time and never looked very good, and I can see that if I had had any sense I would have swept away all the flower beds, abolished the rose bed, moved the honeysuckle and planted a few trees. The former flower beds would have formed part of the lawn, and the rest of it would have been a rough paddock until such time as I had made up my mind what to do with it, and also had the time in which to do it.

If I come straight out and suggest that flower beds are unnecessary, any proper gardener will abandon this book in disgust, but please do not despair. I know that keen gardeners like flower beds more than anything, and they will regard a garden without flower beds as the equivalent of music without instruments (to borrow a phrase from, I think, Bismarck). They know all the names of everything; they love watching the progress of each particular flower or shrub; they cannot pass a garden centre without nipping in to buy something else. They work endlessly and they change things constantly. Now I freely admit that a fine flower bed or a handsome herbaceous border is a very admirable sight, and I always enjoy looking at them, but they require two things: a great deal of work and a certain artistic flair. Whether or not I might grudge the former, I have no claim to the latter, and my efforts at creating flower beds have not gone well. If you are like me, then you have a very good reason for holding out against the pressures of fashion which dictate that you must have a flower bed, or beds, and simply do without.

A minimalist garden has a lot to offer. First of all, a combination of grass and trees can be both pleasant and colourful.

Second, apart from cutting the grass and trimming the hedge, if any, it requires almost no work, and even this you can contract out to someone else if you feel like it.

Third, it will leave you free to grow fruit and vegetables if you so desire and provided you have the space or can rent an allotment. I find this to be a more rewarding activity than fussing over flower beds, and if you want to have flowers for the house you can grow sweet peas or dahlias, or whatever you want, in the vegetable plot, which is the easiest way of doing it.

Fourth, if you happen to be a passionate enthusiast for flower beds, a garden with nothing but trees and grass provides a blank canvas on which you can, so to speak, embroider. (I know nothing about embroidery, but I believe it can be done on canvas.) Having established your minimalist garden, you can, by degrees and at your leisure, add climbers to the walls or pots beside the path, or a rose bed, or even, if you insist, a herbaceous border.

Grass

There are some persuasive people about who will promise to turn your lawn into something worthy of the Chelsea Flower Show. They will come in autumn and feed it with fertilizer and put on stuff which is supposed to kill the moss. They will bring a machine to scratch out the moss, dead or alive. They will feed the grass again in spring, and in summer they will come with weedkiller and try to kill the weeds. All these operations you could carry out for yourself if you had the right equipment and bought the right stuff, and possibly, or even probably, if you or they keep it up year in and year out, you will get a very fine lawn.

I have tried it, and decided it wasn't worth it. The man who came to spray the weeds sprayed some of the flowers by mistake and killed them (which, of course, could not happen in a minimalist garden where there were no flowers). The moss kept coming back, and at the end of a year our lawn did not look any better than my neighbour's, and she had done nothing more to hers than mow it. Our grass now gets mown, but not fed or watered. Occasionally I get a watering can and pour weedkiller on the dandelions and buttercups and daisies, which generally curl up and die. This is known as spot weeding and is quite effective enough for my purposes.

As for mowing, I have been through a good many lawnmowers in my time. Unless you have a very small lawn, the important thing is to get one that is self-propelled, big enough and fast enough. We have one with a Honda engine which is very reliable, but it is about 14 inches wide and moves at about 2 miles an hour, so it takes far too long to mow anything but the smallest patch.

I have, on the other hand, also got an American mower, called a Toro, which is wide and light and very fast to operate. It calls itself a Recycler, which is supposed to mean that you do not need a grass box, and that it will grind the mowings into an invisible dust and scatter them neatly on the lawn, all of which will be good for the grass. In my experience, this does not work. It might work in America in areas where the grass gets very dry and they do not want it cut very short, but if I try the recycling trick the machine deposits a long line of grass mowings which then get tracked into the house, and from time to time it clogs up and stalls. If I use it with a grass box, however, and treat it like an ordinary mower, it works very well. It is truly excellent at cutting the long grass in the chicken run, but unfortunately it refuses to cut the grass on the lawn as short as my wife likes it. For this reason I now get most of the grass cut by someone else.

This is something I heartily recommend. When you look at the price of a good lawnmower, and consider the depreciation on it, and make allowances for having it serviced once a year and occasionally repaired, and also bear in mind the cost of petrol, you may well conclude that the amount that an honest workman would charge you for cutting your grass represents a very favourable bargain, and furthermore you will be helping a respectable fellow to earn a decent living.

All of this supposes that you have got some grass to cut. If you have to start at the beginning with bare earth and grass seed, I can only help you by repeating the rather patronising story of the American lady who asked a gardener at Hampton Court to tell her the secret of such wonderful lawns.

'Ar,' he said. (All gardeners start by saying 'Ar' in this situation.) 'First you dig it.

Then you level it.

Then you rake it.

Then you sow it.

Then you roll it... and you mow it...

for hundreds and hundreds of years.'

Trees

There is no need for a minimalist garden to be short of colour, because there is a lot of colour in trees. Unless you have a very large garden, these have to be trees that grow only to a reasonable size, not potentially enormous oaks or ashes or limes. We have a young horse chestnut which I have grown from a conker, and this will one day be too big for our garden so I have planted it on the verge by the road outside. As it is very slow growing the benefit will be felt by posterity and not by me, and I shall be surprised if I live to see it bloom. Otherwise our garden-size trees include those with glorious purple leaves, such as the Japanese maple and the *Prunus*; our whitebeam with a kind of silvery sheen to it, and little white flowers in spring; a flowering almond that flowers at all sorts of times, and the pink may tree which puts on a fine show in early summer. We get beautiful apple blossom from the Bramley, and less beautiful plum blossom from the Victoria. Unless the frost gets them they produce fruit, which is a good thing but may mean that the grass in that area gets covered with rotting fruit in which wasps like to lurk with a view to stinging the legs of passing children.

We also have a magnolia, which my father gave us because of a conversation which took place in his presence when he was a boy. 'I do wish,' said my grandmother, 'that I had a magnolia.'

'My dear, you shall,' said my grandfather, and, ordering the horse to be put to the trap, drove out and bought one. I never knew either my grandfather or my grandmother, but this was considered by my father to be the only faintly romantic gesture that my grandfather ever made, and so he gave us a magnolia to commemorate the event.

One of the pleasures of this type of garden lies in sitting in the shade of trees and watching the blue tits and chaffinches and nuthatches and the green-and-red woodpeckers and the black-and-white woodpeckers which come to eat the peanuts and the sunflower seeds which we hang out for them. For this purpose our trees are more or less in the right place. The planting of trees has something in common with educating children, by which I mean that it is pretty awkward if you get it wrong. If you put a child into the wrong school, you can probably move him or her if you get on with it quickly, but it is no good waiting until the child is eighteen and then wishing you had sent him or her somewhere else. Similarly, if you plant a tree in the wrong place you can shift it while it is young, but if, when it is fully grown, you realize that it is throwing its shade in the wrong place, there is nothing much you can do beyond cut it down. When planting, therefore, you need to look ahead and choose the site with care, considering especially where the shade will be at different times of day. In our case, we have to sit where the whitebeam throws its shade, rather than where we would like it to throw it, and where it would throw it if we had planted it about 4 yards further back.

The trees to avoid above all others are poplars, unless you can put them very well away from any buildings. When we moved into our house there was a line of young poplars along the inadequate fence that I mentioned earlier, presumably planted as a windbreak as we are much exposed to the south wind. They were very nice poplars. They made a gentle sighing and rustling sound in the breeze, which was restful. At the end of summer they produced a sort of feathery cotton wool which floated onto the lawn and was a bit of a nuisance but didn't matter much as it got collected up with the grass by the lawnmower. Without our noticing, these poplars got bigger every year and then in the dry summer of 1976 a crack appeared in the side of our house.

I sent for a surveyor, who said that the problem lay with the poplar trees, which must, he declared, be cut down at once. As the trees were over 20 yards from the house, the rest of the family said the roots could not possibly extend so far, that the surveyor was obviously mad, the poplar trees entirely innocent, and that I should take no notice. I said, on the other hand, that I was not going to pay the man's bill and ignore his advice, so I sent for a woodsman and had them felled. As a result, I can tell you that a mature poplar does not let go of its hold on life without a struggle. Every stump sent up new shoots, as happens in the process known as coppicing. After the trees were felled, each trunk was cut into shorter pieces, and each piece tried to become a tree in its own right, by sending out both shoots and roots. All across the lawn suckers sprang up from the original roots, some of them appearing right against the wall of the house and so proving the surveyor to have been absolutely right.

I mowed the tops off the suckers in the lawn, poisoned the stumps with weedkiller, and eventually the rains came, the crack closed, and the surveyor came back to assure me that everything was now all right and I need do no more. Which cautionary tale I make a point of telling because, when I cycled across Ireland, I kept seeing an attractive little tree planted in small gardens which proved to be *Populus candicans* 'Aurora'. If this particular poplar behaves like our poplars, then there are going to be lots of houses in Ireland with cracks in the wall.

Climbers, Pots, and Advertising Copywriters

If you are going to bring any further embroidery into a minimalist garden, the least troublesome way to do it is either with climbers or with pots, or possibly both. I said earlier that our garden came with a useless archway covered with honeysuckle, so I scrapped the archway and moved the honeysuckle up against the garage. Fifty years later it is in a most flourishing state. When flowering, it looks good and greets you with a delicious whiff of honeysuckle scent as you walk down the path to the front door. It is fixed to the garage wall with a discreet loop of plastic rope, and needs to be clipped if it gets too big, but otherwise gives no trouble.

We also have a winter-flowering jasmine near the door, which somebody gave us as a cutting, and I rather wish they hadn't. I suppose gardeners in general suffer from other gardeners giving them things, and I have been struggling for years against a beastly orange thing called montbretia which will take over a whole bed if you let it, and which arrived as a present from a well-intentioned friend. The jasmine is by no means as bad as the montbretia, and indeed those coming to the front door always like the smell when it is in flower. They do not like it if it is raining as it then drips on them, and it also gets very big and is rather tiresome to prune and to tie up. Also it looks pretty dead a lot of the time, so I am not sure that I would not be happier without it.

Then there are climbing roses, but roses are such a big subject that I will give them a section on their own, which I will come to shortly, and will now go on to pots.

In spite of the bother of watering, things in pots are easier to manage than things in the ground, chiefly because they do not need much weeding, or so it seems to me. I really took up pots after I first went to Greece, because the Greeks are great people for growing things in pots, or even in old olive-oil tins painted red, or something else along those lines. Geraniums are favourites with the Greek nation, which is understandable bearing in mind that they stand heat very well and drought pretty well and come in lots of glorious colours. The frost kills them off over here, and I used to take cuttings and overwinter them on window sills, which cluttered the house up and is a bit of a bore. You can buy forty or so 'plug plants' in

spring for not much money, which is a lot less bother and forty geraniums at three or four to the pot will fill enough pots for anyone. I also get a couple of trailing fuchsias, and these I have found by experiment do not seem to like to be under a south wall, where they wither and look miserable, but are as cheerful as anything under a north wall. This you may find useful information if you have got a north wall. Then we have oleanders.

The reason we have oleanders is that, like geraniums, they grow very freely and look very fine in Greece, and Greece is a country we are both keen on. Somebody gave us an oleander some time ago, but it never flowered and quickly died, so we thought that oleanders would not do over here. Then, last spring, we read a persuasive advertisement which offered us, at a knock-down price, three oleanders said to be tough, adaptable and impervious to frost, so we sent off for them. They came with a leaflet which, contrary to the advertisement, made it plain that oleanders were among the more fragile and delicate of plants which could really only be grown successfully in a special compost and in pots of a huge dimension. The suppliers further suggested that I should give them some more money to buy overcoats of 'breathable fleece' for each one to wear and keep itself warm in a frost.

There was no going back, so I went and bought three huge plastic pots and got the ingredients for the special compost, and I mixed it up and planted them according to instructions. I am pleased to say that they are, at the time of writing, flowering in an attractive manner. In Greece the oleanders seem to flower all through the summer, but I wait to see how long these ones keep growing if grown in pots in England. As for the frost, I propose to put them under the window in the garage for the winter, and hope that they manage without breathable fleeces. I may add that the instructions which came with them say that I should wear gloves whenever I touch them as the sap is 'very toxic'. They don't say exactly how toxic, but I have never heard that there is a high mortality rate from oleander poisoning among the children and goats of Greece, so perhaps they are sublethally toxic.

In connection with the oleander advertisement, I will here deviate from the main purpose of this book in order to say something about advertising copywriters in general and horticultural copywriters in particular. I have twice mentioned Greece in the past few pages, and some of the world's finest copywriters are employed by the Greek National Tourism Organisation. If you go to their London office and pick up a leaflet on any part of Greece, you will get the impression that, in its way, that particular area surpasses anywhere else in the world except for other parts of Greece, the countryside in each case being generally superior to the Garden of Eden, and the buildings a decided advance upon those of anywhere you care to mention. This is impressive, and shows a lively imagination, but I do not rate these copywriters quite as highly as those employed by mail-order wine merchants.

I was for a time regularly bombarded with letters most kindly letting me into such secrets as that somewhere in the choicest parts of the Rhône valley they had stumbled upon a parcel of 250 cases of the finest wine that you could ever imagine, which had somehow been overlooked by the grower in the course of his normal business. This parcel they had cunningly persuaded him to part with at a most favourable price, and with astonishing generosity they offered it to me at £7.99 the bottle, against the £12.99 it would easily command in the open market. I should, they said, move quickly, as they expected this lot to go off like hot cakes, but it never seemed to matter if I missed any particular opportunity, as within a matter of days a fresh letter would arrive to let me know of another amazing scoop by way of a quite extraordinary bargain from somewhere else, such as the banks of the Loire.

Gardening copywriters write in much the same style. They rarely acknowledge anything other than perfection in anything they offer, and they have photographs to prove their point. Every plant will produce a profusion of blooms or a cornucopia of fruit, and from their seeds vegetables the like of which you have never tasted will spring into being with the minimum of trouble. As for keeping up with the Joneses, those wretched people will be ill with envy when they see the state of your garden.

What actually happens when you buy their stuff is generally rather different, as I have said in connection with the oleanders, and as seems to be the case with my blueberries. Blueberries arrived on the garden scene suddenly. We knew that they made them into pies in America, but nobody seemed to grow them over here. Then, all at once, the nurserymen of Britain took them up, and set their copywriters to work to compose lyrical essays on the merits of the luscious blueberry, backed with colour photographs of bushes in a state of collapse under the weight of the fruit. I do not consider myself to be a particularly gullible man, but prefer to think that I have a trusting nature, which unfortunately means that I am an easy victim of practical jokers and copywriters. Anyway, I put my trust in blueberries and bought two plants of different varieties because the copywriters said this was best for pollination. They also said I should plant them in large pots filled with ericaceous compost (suitable for such things as azaleas and rhododendrons), so I did that as well.

In the first year one variety flowered and the other did not. The one with flowers did not seem to mind not being pollinated by the other, but produced fruit, to a total of about ten small blueberries. In the second year they both flowered, and one ripened about eight good sized blueberries, a bit smaller than the smallest of marbles, while the other did better in number, to a total of some twenty-four, the berries being about the size of large peas. None of them seemed to taste of anything very much, and all they have been good for so far is to add a little decorative colour to bowls of other fruit, such as raspberries. I suppose in fairness I should wait for another year or two before bringing in a final verdict, but I am at present inclined to say that the blueberry represents a further triumph of the copywriter's art.

Roses, Rock Roses, Sweet Peas and the Border

Many if not most gardens have their strong points. In one garden you may think the azaleas and rhododendrons are wonderful and in another that the dahlias are splendid. In our garden, if you were to think such thoughts at all, it would be about the roses or the rock roses, or just possibly the sweet peas. Furthermore, I need to explain that I have dealt successfully with the herbaceous border by means of the management technique known as Delegation.

Roses

I suppose that when the genetic engineers get around to roses they will make them available growing on their own roots, to whatever height you like, of whatever colour you choose, each with a heavenly scent, all immune to black spot, mildew or rust, and the whole impervious to attack from greenfly, thrips and that invisible creature which gnaws the buds and may be an earwig for all I know. Until such time as rose growing has been de-skilled in this way, to produce really good roses will require a certain amount of trouble.

Having said which, I do believe that the modern hybrid tea rose is one of the greatest achievements in the history of plant breeding. They come in wonderful colours and with wonderful scents. If you treat them fairly they flower bravely, then have a slight lull, and flower again. I rate them higher than floribundas because they put on just as good a general show with better individual blooms. Old roses are all very well on their day, but they only flower once and then pack up until next year. The only varieties to run hybrid teas close are the David Austin roses, which tend to have an old-fashioned rosette shape to them, but are modern in other ways. You can indeed mix hybrid teas and David Austins to good effect in the same bed, and the only other types I would consider at all are the little China roses, which are very good for buttonholes if you go in for buttonholes, and for small arrangements on the dining table.

We have a fine round bed of hybrid tea roses, and I believe that it is best, if you have enough room, to grow them in a bed of their own, rather than as part of a mixed border. In our case there is a bird bath in the middle and a border of lavender round the edge, and it all looks particularly sensational when the lavender is in bloom, at which time the scent is wonderful. I have some others that I grow for cutting in the vegetable bed, and the great thing about all these roses is that they are planted in black stuff, which is something I most heartily recommend.

This black stuff ought to have a proper name, but the roll I bought from the ironmonger just says it is 100% UV Stabilised Spun-Bonded Polypropylene, so there. Anyway it is a black plastic which lets the water through but keeps the weeds down. What I had not reckoned on, but was delighted to find, is that it also stops suckers. Most roses are budded onto briars, rather than grown on their own roots, and the briar is never content with this humble role, but keeps asserting itself by sending up suckers which would be dog roses if they could. To stop them taking over you usually have to scrabble about with a knife, or possibly a pruning saw, cutting them out at ground level and getting scratched in the process. With roses grown in black stuff there seem to be no suckers, so all that is avoided.

You get a bed ready for planting by digging and hoeing and raking and all that, and unroll the black stuff over it, burying it at the edge and overlapping it as necessary, so that the whole bed is covered. Then you cut an X where you want to plant and scoop out a hole deep enough to let you plant the rose so that the top of the briar stem is just above the ground. Plant the rose; put back the earth you have scooped out, mixing in a handful of bonemeal, and close the black stuff round the rose. When you have planted the whole bed, cover it with bark chips, which look better and stop the black stuff from perishing in the sunlight. I have made that sound quite simple, and I believe that it is, but honesty compels me to admit that our rose-cum-lavender bed was planted for us by a professional whom we engaged to do it. However, I have grown other things in black stuff successfully, and the only special thing that I can see about roses is that you need a deeper hole for the roots than you do for, say, strawberries. The professional did it as I have described, but I believe she got a heavy type of black stuff which she said was called Mytex, and you might have to hunt around a bit to find a source.

The process of planting comes after the process of choosing, and you can have a happy time browsing the catalogues of rose growers to see which you like the look and sound of. These catalogues will tell you roughly what height they will grow to, and which have the best scent, and will drop you a hint as to which are particularly likely to get black spot or mildew. The catalogue I have before me has some symbols which they say means that 'disease resistance' is either Very Good, Good or Average. It is, of course, mathematically impossible for everything to be Average or above, so there ought to be some described as Bad and Very Bad, but there aren't. Of the fifty-one hybrid teas which they illustrate, forty-nine are said to be Very Good at disease resistance, two to be Average, and none to be Good. The lesson here is to avoid anything that is not Very Good, and not to pin too much hope on that description, because in most years pretty well all roses will get some degree of black spot and mildew towards the end of summer.

The symbol for disease resistance in this catalogue is a picture of a greenfly, which is nonsense as a greenfly is not a disease but an insect. In my experience if greenfly attack at all, they attack all roses impartially, but some roses, especially pink ones, seem to be particularly attractive to thrips.

There is one quality in a rose which I regard as most desirable and which catalogues never seem to mention, namely that it should last well in water. There is a beautiful rose called Sutter's Gold which is easy to grow, has a wonderful scent, produces blooms of a perfect shape, but if you put it in a vase just as it is opening, in twenty-four hours it will be blown. From my observation those roses that last well as cut flowers do everything in slow motion, which is logical when you come to think about it. They tend to flower rather late, the buds take longer to open than most, and once open they outlast other roses in the bed. As the catalogues never give you any clues about this, it is best to visit a nursery if you can and make some enquiries. Rose growers are like antique dealers in that they will generally give you an honest answer to a direct question, so if you ask what faults may lurk in any particular variety, and which have the merit of growing in slow motion, you could get useful information beyond what they put in their catalogues. I need hardly remind you that the catalogues are written by copywriters.

Pruning

Some years ago there was a report in the papers that the Royal Horticultural Society, or possibly the Royal National Rose Society, had carried out an experiment by pruning one lot of rose bushes lightly, another lot heavily, and by way of control, cutting down a third group with a hedge cutter. To the great surprise of one and all, those hacked off with the hedge cutter did the best, from which the moral is that if you have both courage and a hedge cutter you could lop the whole lot down to what looks to you to be a suitable size. I have the hedge cutter but not the courage, so I do it with secateurs in the traditional way.

With hybrid teas I prune twice. In the autumn, when all flowering is over, I cut out all dead wood and spindly little growths, and then shorten the main stems so that they do not rock about too much in the wind. I make sure that nothing is higher than the bird bath in the middle of the bed, which is, to be precise, 30 inches. Then in March, when growth is about to start, I prune them some more, where possible cutting to an outward eye, i.e. where a group of leaves join the stem. Roses are surprisingly well able to stand hard pruning, but all the same it is possible to kill off a really vigorous rose by cutting it back too much, and I get nervous about this. Accordingly I do not cut the naturally tall varieties as low as the shorter ones, but after this second pruning they will all be below the bird bath, from which you will be able to deduce that I have pruned them down to under 30 inches.

Pruning climbers is a different matter. These I prune once a year, in the autumn. I cut out the dead wood, take the top off any main stems that have got too long, and shorten the side shoots to about 9 inches.

Cutting

Then there is the matter of cutting them during the summer, either because the flowers are dead or because you want them fresh for the house. I recommend you to cut them on a principle explained to me by a Dutchman. This Dutchman was a professional grower of roses, and in my opinion the views of such Dutchmen are to be taken seriously. As he explained, the leaves on a rose stem usually come in fives or in threes, and when cutting back, cut back fairly hard to a point just above a five, where there is also another five below that. The idea is that the eyes are stronger where there are five leaves, and so with luck you will get two fresh shoots, one from the joint just below your cut, and the other from the joint below that. If you cannot understand what I have written, I think it will become clear when you look at a stem.

Feeding

I feed all roses three times a year. In autumn, after the first pruning, I scatter a handful of bonemeal and a pinch of dried seaweed round each one. The bonemeal is standard practice, but the seaweed an improvement of my own, as I am an ardent believer in seaweed for reasons explained later. Then in April I give them a small handful of some proprietary rose fertilizer, and a second such handful in July or August when the first flowering is over.

Spraying

A now-deceased friend who was an apple grower by profession told me that there is no point in spraying apple trees at all unless you are prepared to spray them at least ten times during the summer. Something similar is true of roses. In the case both of apples and of roses, you spray mainly to prevent fungal diseases. As grown by professionals, the Cox's Orange Pippin has been transformed from a cracked and horrid-looking apple into a smooth attractive fruit by regular spraying against apple scab. The enemies in the case of roses are principally black spot and mildew, and it is not much use waiting until one of these attacks as once the spores get hold it is pretty well impossible to dislodge them, or so it seems to me. It says in the book that you should pull off all leaves affected with black spot or rust, gather up all those that have fallen on the ground, and burn them, but I have never found that this makes the slightest difference. Once started, black spot seems to keep going until the end of the season.

My efforts at defeating it start at dead of winter. When everything is dormant, I make a mixture of 2 ounces of Jeyes Fluid in 2 gallons of water and slosh it all over the rose bed. I tried spraying it on but it wrecked the sprayer, by somehow splitting the lance, so now I do it with the watering can, the intention being to kill off any overwintering spores. A pharmacist acquaintance poured scorn on this idea as he said that Jeyes Fluid would rapidly be inactivated by the organic matter on the ground. As he was a very clever fellow I am ready to believe that he is right, so I try to wet the stems of the roses as much as possible, rather than the ground. Anyway, it does no harm, as a preliminary to spraying with a fungicide once a fortnight through the summer.

This I start in April as the first shoots appear, and I keep it up as long as the bushes are flowering. It seems to me that black spot starts at the bottom and works its way up, so I spray the lower leaves with special care, wetting them above and below. Mildew, on the other hand, seems to appear higher up, so you need to spray the higher leaves as well.

Greenfly is the most common insect pest, but because of the danger to bees and to other benevolent creatures such as ladybirds, I spray only when necessary, rather than as a routine. It is just a matter of keeping an eye on the plants and spraying as soon as greenfly appear.

The dreaded thrips are sometimes known as thunder flies, because they seem to strike in hot muggy weather, and in these circumstances I may give a precautionary spray to those grown for cutting, but I leave the main bed alone unless positive symptoms appear.

As to what sprays to use, it would be unwise for me to offer advice as some things disappear off the market and new things come on, and I may well recommend a spray that no longer exists by the time this book comes out. I will nevertheless risk saying that I find the fungicide which is called Systhane Fungus Fighter to be very good against black spot and mildew. There are those who have a childlike faith in spraying greenfly with soap and water in the belief that this will drown them, which in my experience it doesn't. You can choose a proprietary insecticide which boasts of its Green, organic and generally harmless properties, but I find these also to be harmless to the creatures they are meant to kill, so I can only suggest that you look along the shelf in the ironmongers or garden centre and choose some poison which somehow persuades you that it might do the job.

Helianthemums, otherwise Rock Roses

Lawrence D. Hills, whose name is much revered by organic gardeners, he being a sort of patron saint of the Green movement, wrote a book called *Down to Earth*

Fruit and Vegetable Growing, which I bought in 1960. The most useful pages had nothing to do with either fruit or vegetables but were about helianthemums. These, he said, could be planted in drifts and would 'blaze through June and July as the most colourful weed-suppressing plant'. On the south side of our house there is a wide gravel path and I thought it might be a bright idea to plant helianthemums up against the house wall, so I did. I see that I noted in the Hills book that I bought a dozen plants from Southview Nurseries of Eversley Cross, Hants, at a cost of seven shillings and sixpence. Some fifty years later they are still doing fine and I don't see why they shouldn't go on forever. They start to blaze earlier than he says, from mid May in fact, and have become, as L. D. Hills has it, 'a colourful drift'. Their weed-suppressing powers are not perfect, but they are very little trouble to look after, especially as, after they have flowered, I set the lawnmower high and mow their tops off, which is easier than clipping them, as L. D. Hills says you should. I have never come across a drift of helianthemums growing anywhere else, which is surprising as it looks great when the flowers are out, and is a tidy green mass otherwise.

Sweet Peas

I regard these as something to be grown in the vegetable bed, as the sticks that are needed to support them are not very sightly, until they get hidden by flowers, but I will deal with sweet peas here for the benefit of those who have no vegetable bed.

Sweet pea seed catalogues are almost as enticing as rose catalogues, and you can spend a long time trying to decide between the Beautifully Scented, the Superb for Cutting, the Show Bench Winner, or the Classic Large Blooms. If you get several varieties you will get far too many seeds, as there are usually twenty in a packet, nearly all of which will germinate. I find that eighteen plants, once they get going, will give us more than all the flowers we need, with quite a lot to give away.

You can sow them in autumn or in spring, and there are two approved ways of growing them. The simplest is to provide the plants with canes, pea sticks or netting and just let them get on with it, tying them in occasionally if necessary. Then there is a more complicated and laborious alternative, in which you grow them up single canes and restrict them to one main stem per plant by pulling off all the side shoots (but not the young flower stems). This method gives you flowers with lovely long stems, but the snag is that the plants grow with astonishing speed and soon reach the tops of the canes. Then it says in the book that you must take each one down, lay it along the ground, lead it along and start it climbing up a cane some distance away from where its roots are. I have tried this, and it does not work, or at least not in my hands, because when I take them down and try to lead them to a new position they simply break. Having abandoned this approach, I now recommend the following:

- Buy a single packet of a variety called Jet Set. It says on the packet that they will grow to about 3 feet tall but on my method they grow to about 7.

- Sow them in October. The first step is to tip the seeds into a saucer, pour in enough water so that they are about half covered, and put them on a windowsill with something over the top, such as a magazine, so that they are in the dark. After a few days they will sprout, and then the best plan is to sow them in compost individually, in things called Rootrainers which you can get from garden centres. Alternatively, though it is not quite so good, you can sow them in 5-inch pots at five to the pot.

- Put them in a cold frame over the winter. If you haven't got a cold frame or an unheated greenhouse I don't see why they shouldn't start growing under the window inside a shed or garage, and later you could rig them up some sort of protection with polythene or even a pane of glass, and put them outside. They are pretty hardy, but can succumb to a really hard frost, especially if you over-water them. Once each plant has four pairs of leaves, pinch out the top, which will cause it to grow strong, fresh shoots from below.

🌹 Plant them out in April, at a time when no sharp frost is forecast. Cut a strip of black stuff (see roses) 18 inches wide and bury each end, weighting down the middle here and there with a brick or log. Put in 7-foot bamboo poles along each side of the black stuff, 9 inches apart, each one opposite another. Cross them and tie them about a foot from the top, as for runner beans. Then put a bean stick or something similar in the V at the top, and tie each pair of canes to it. You also need to brace the whole structure against the wind, which is most easily done by banging in stakes opposite each end cane and tying these canes to them. Then I drape ordinary pea netting over the whole thing to give them something to hang on to when they start growing seriously. If you haven't got room for a row like that you can make a wigwam, or wigwams, of canes and grow them up it (or them).

🌹 Put one plant by each cane, putting a teaspoonful of bonemeal and a pinch of seaweed in the hole. Then firm them in, give them some slug bait, and forget them.

For a long time they will do nothing but sit there, occasionally looking miserable after a frost, but in the end they will get going properly. At first you need to tie them to the canes, but after a bit they will start to grip the netting for themselves. You will have to weed them occasionally, but the black stuff will put a stop to weeds in the middle.

Now come the two clever bits. First, remove the side shoots (but not the young flower stems) in the way I described earlier. This is not all that laborious, and you do not need to be fanatical about it, but keep an eye on them, and where you see side shoots developing, pull them off. The plants will almost certainly defeat you by sometimes escaping notice and growing side shoots on the sly, but this does not matter much. Also they will put up fresh stems from near the ground, and one or two of these you can let grow, but keep pulling off side shoots whenever you spot them.

What you can expect to get is, at first, some fine flowers on long stalks, and later a mass of sweet peas on shorter stalks. All of these are very desirable, and Jet Set will not grow tall enough to require that business of taking them down from one cane and trying to get them to grow up another.

The second clever bit is a matter of little black flies. At some point in the summer you will almost certainly find that when you bring a bunch of sweet peas into the house, a lot of tiny black creatures drop off and start crawling about. This is not pleasant. I have tried spraying the plants and found this to be entirely useless. I have also tried plunging the flowers, after I have picked them, into a bucket of detergent and water in the hope that this will drown the black creatures, which it does not. Then I heard from a friend that a professional grower, possibly a Dutchman, had advised her to pick the sweet peas and put them in a dark corner of some shed or garage, leaving the door or a window open. The black creatures, he said, would leave en masse and fly to the light. We have a stable with no window, so I put a bunch of sweet peas in a shady part one evening, left the top of the stable door open, and when I came to collect them next morning, behold – all the black flies had flown. Anyone who has bought this book will have got value for money if they grow sweet peas and did not know this tip already.

The Border

Having written at some length on the merits of not having a herbaceous border, I must now confess that we have got one. It has a history. We had a pretty poor version of such a thing which seemed to take up a lot of my time with nothing satisfactory to show for it. Then for our fiftieth wedding anniversary we decided that we would give each other a lovely new border by way of a mutual present, to be laid out and maintained by a professional. Accordingly we got a garden designer who made a plan, enlarged the existing bed, threw out a lot of old things and planted all sorts of new things. The intention was that she should come back for some hours every month to make sure it all looked lovely, but such is life that she fell in love, got married, became pregnant and disappeared. The bed thus lapsed back into my hands, taking even more of my time as it was now larger. It began to show signs of falling back into something like its former state, but we now have the services of a gardener called Dominic, who comes for an hour a week, regular as clockwork.

At the beginning of our relationship I spoke to him as follows:

'Dominic, that bed is your affair. I wash my hands of it. Make of it what you will. I wish to have nothing to do with it beyond looking at it.'

As things have developed, that is still pretty much the way it is, except that I do spray the two climbing and three bush roses in this bed when I am spraying all the others. Also Dominic and I have occasional conversations about it which tend to start by my saying something like:

'There is too much yellow. Can we have more pinks and blues and reds?'
'This or that is getting smothered/is in a silly place. What about moving it?'

My role is really no more than to make an occasional tentative suggestion – an arrangement which has taken a great load off my mind, and the bed is coming along nicely in Dominic's hands, and getting to look pretty good.

The result of all this activity is that, year after year, I get much to look forward to. It is, of course, in the nature of flowers to have this effect. In January I can look forward to the first primroses in the hedges, and once the primroses are out, I can look forward to the bluebells in the woods. In the garden, when the rock roses start to flower I look forward to the roses coming out, and when the roses begin to come out I look forward to picking sweet peas. Something similar happens in respect of Dominic's border. When the daffodils are out I begin to look for the tulips, and when the tulips are out, I stand by for the paeonies and the poppies. All in all, it is a most satisfactory arrangement.

The Tool Shed, Chemicals and the Organic Question

There is a certain type of man to whom a well-stocked ironmonger's shop is like an art gallery. Such men get enormous pleasure from displays of hammers of different types and sizes hung up on racks as if they were pictures, and they like to browse among spanners and saws, and to admire tidy little boxes filled with gleaming screws of one sort and another. To such a man his workshop or tool shed is his own modest collection, which he keeps in beautiful order and to which he likes to retreat like a bibliophile to his library or a collector to his stamps.

I am not that sort of person, but I confess that I have come to understand the feeling since I discovered Tool

Hooks. I have, over fifty years, accumulated a good number of gardening tools, and they used to be all over the place, some in the garden shed, some in the garage and some in the stable which doubles as a woodshed now that all the ponies have departed. Some tools hung on nails, some leant against the wall, and if I wanted three different items at the same time, they often seemed to be in three different places. Then I discovered Tool Hooks in the village ironmonger, and now the garden shed is an impressively tidy affair, with spade and fork, rake and shears all hanging tastefully around the walls on little tin Tool Hooks, with the sprayer suspended in the corner. I get a certain amount of feel-good factor every time I look at them and have something of the sensations of a connoisseur.

There are three items which I regard as the pick of my collection, none of which can be bought from a garden centre or ironmonger. One I got from the Internet, one I bought in the flea market in Athens, and one I invented and had made to order.

The Hori-hori

When I say I got one from the Internet, the strict truth is that Dominic the gardener got it for me as I don't do Internet. I noticed that he had one, and asked him to get one for me. I expect that you cannot get them in garden centres because the police would probably close down any establishment that stocked them, and I find it surprising that trafficking in them on the Internet is allowed.

The hori-hori is a Japanese knife. It looks to be the sort of thing that a Japanese with suicidal tendencies would keep handy for purposes of hara-kiri. It has a wooden handle, a broad but sharply pointed and slightly hollow blade, with a cutting edge on either side. It has a label with Japanese hieroglyphics on the handle and there are more hieroglyphics on the leather sheath which comes with it. This sheath you can hang on your belt, and I should think that if you wore it in any public place it would get you several years in prison.

Its use is for weeding. You can use it with a thrusting action of the point, like a rapier (possibly exclaiming 'hori-hori' as you do so, in the manner of a samurai warrior), or you can employ a slashing action of the edges, like a cutlass.

It is so effective that I almost feel it is unfair to the weeds, as they simply do not stand a chance against the hori-hori.

The Mattock

I do not know either the Greek or the English name for the tool that I bought in the Athens flea market, so I call it a mattock, which, strictly speaking, it isn't. My *Chambers Everyday Dictionary* defines a mattock as 'a kind of pickaxe for loosening the soil, having one or both of the iron ends broad instead of pointed'. My pseudo-mattock is like a true mattock but with only one broad end and with no point, being therefore roughly like a very heavy draw hoe on a pick handle. It is superb for loosening the soil, as Chambers says, and as a tool to clear a large area of weeds it is quicker and easier to use than a hoe, and as a means of surface cultivation it is quicker and easier than a spade or fork. I have never seen one in a shop in England but there are plenty to be had in the Athens flea market.

The Driber

This, the tool which I have invented, is in essence a long-handled dibber. You drive it into the ground with your foot, and so I call it a Driber as a sort of amalgam of the word dibber and the word driver. A dibber is, of course, a little thing of about 14 inches long, in the shape of a T with a point at one end, made of wood but often with the point cased in iron. Its use is for making holes for planting things. My Driber, on the other hand, is made to the proportions of a spade, by which I mean that it is 38 inches long and has a T-shaped handle and a crossbar 28 inches below the handle. It differs from a spade in that, below the crossbar, instead of a broad blade it has a pointed end 10 inches long. The whole is made of galvanized iron piping, because I happened to have some of this which I took to a local engineer and asked him to make me a Driber.

The advantages of a Driber over a dibber are:

🌹 That you do not have to bend double or crouch down to use it.

🌹 That you can drive it into the ground with the weight of your foot.

🌹 That it is useful for making holes for fixing stakes as well as for planting things.

If you want to plant potatoes, you do it by driving in the Driber and then enlarging the hole by swinging the handle round in an arc. To plant leeks, you press it in to the full extent of the point and drop the plants in. For lettuce plants you do not press it in so far and so make shallower holes. When it comes to staking things like dahlias, or putting in bean sticks for runner beans, the Driber will make you a hole 10 inches long to take the stake. I find it invaluable.

I showed my mark 1 Driber to a retired Royal Engineer friend who was so taken with it that he made himself a mark 2 version, slightly different in that it had a wooden end instead of a metal point. He painted it nicely and it looked much better than mine, so I asked him to make me eight more. Of these I kept one, gave one away, and persuaded the local ironmonger to take six on sale or return terms. He said to me cheerfully 'everything sells in the end' which may be a feature of the ironmongery business, but anyway they did sell, and this was encouraging. I hope his customers were satisfied, but they may not have been because of the wooden ends. These may be satisfactory for the light soil of my friend's garden, but it isn't on our heavy soil and when I used the mark 2 version, the end broke. From this I conclude that Dribers of the future must be metal throughout, like the mark 1.

Having reached this point, I could see that if I were a man of dash and go I would contrive to get a quantity of Dribers made in stainless steel in China as the mark 3 version and then ask to go on that television programme called *Dragons' Den*. In case you have not seen this programme, I will tell you that a succession of people with some idea or invention appear before a panel of millionaires and try to persuade one or more of them to put some of his or her millions into the idea or invention in question. The millionaires generally behave in a disagreeable manner and I have noticed that they are not so much impressed by a really clever product as by a really slick sales pitch from the inventor. From this I conclude that the millionaires are basically conmen, as I have observed in life that one conman will generally fall for the con trick of another.

My approach would at least be unusual, because I would start like this:

'Now then, you Dragons, I notice that people usually come on this programme to ask for a hundred thousand pounds of your money and offer a twenty per cent share in their company. I don't want anything like that, but I am prepared to accept fifteen pounds from any one of you who is interested in my product. In return I will let you have a specimen of the item in question; the fifteen pounds is non-returnable, but at that price you are getting a bargain. You may take it away and do any testing and costing and pricing and market research, and any other boring activities you feel to be necessary and with which I cannot be bothered. If, after that, you want to market it, you can come back and we will discuss the question of a royalty. I shall, of course, assign my rights to whoever offers me the highest royalty, unless it happens that I have taken a dislike to whoever turns out to be the highest bidder.' (I say this because it seems to me that the Dragons quite often turn people down not because there is anything wrong with their proposal, but because they have taken against the proposer.)

I will then proceed like this:

'In case any of you are not gardeners, I will start by showing you a dibber.' (Of course they aren't gardeners. I do not suppose that any one of these millionaires would get his or her hands dirty in a garden.) Anyway, I would go on from there, and they could ask me anything they liked, and I am confident that in the end they would all say 'I'm out', this being the standard phrase they use to dash the hopes of aspiring entrepreneurs.

A weakness of my proposal is that I have no patent on the Driber, and on so simple a device I probably could not get one if I tried. Even if I might be able to patent it, I was put off the idea of trying by an inventor I met, who I think may have been the man who invented the Tool Hook. 'Patents,' he said 'are a very devil. Once you register a patent you have to spend thousands of pounds defending it from all the people who will try to get round it.' As that is not a pleasant or practicable way for me to spend my remaining years, I have not made any approach to a patent agent or the Patent Office. This being so, I am sure that the Dragons, supposing that they were bright enough to recognize the full merits of the Driber, would also be sufficiently sharp to spot this weakness and see that there is no earthly reason why they should pay me a royalty. It would be much simpler for them just to steal the idea and get on with it.

This would be one reason for turning me down, but there is another even more compelling. From what I have seen of the Dragons, their idea is always that someone else should do the work and they should cream off a good slice of the profit. My proposal, that they themselves should take on the hard labour, is hardly likely to appeal. For which reason I have not been in touch with the television people in the hope of going on the programme. As you might say, 'I'm out.'

To bring this matter to a conclusion, let me say that the way is open. Any gardener who wants a Driber may get one made for himself, and any enterprising entrepreneur who can see its potential may go ahead and launch the Driber upon the world to the benefit of gardeners everywhere.

My Short Stick

As well as these three, which I prize above the rest of my collection, a home-made tool I use regularly is a stick exactly 2 feet long with a notch precisely in the middle. Seed packets and gardening books constantly say things like 'Sow in double rows 1 foot apart, 8 inches between seeds' or 'Sow in drills 15 inches apart and thin to 6 inches between plants'. Of course you can always guess, but my stick comes in useful for getting it right.

Chemicals

When I look back to the early years of my gardening life I am astonished at the range of toxic chemicals which we were all encouraged to use. DDT, when it first appeared, was greeted as a wonderful and useful thing which would slaughter pretty well any insect or mite you can think of. As well as massacring malarial mosquitoes in the jungly parts of the world, it was thought to be useful stuff for us to spray around the house from aerosols or slosh upon the plants in our garden. I think I am right in saying that it earned its discoverer the Nobel Prize. Then there came a substance called lindane, which I think may have been a chemically similar but somehow superior version of DDT. After a time these two began to work less well because the insects got resistant to them, and they were succeeded by the organophosphorus compounds, these being derivatives from the poisonous nerve gases which the Nazis developed during the war. I recall one called malathion which had a foul smell and formed the active basis of a great many garden insecticides. I am sure that, at different times, I have had little bottles in the tool shed with the contents based on DDT, on lindane, or on malathion.

There were many other chemicals restricted to farmers, such as those called aldrin and dieldrin which were used to control soil pests, and the whole burgeoning agricultural chemical industry was going great guns, when everything changed. Many of these chemicals were found to do great harm to the soil and to wildlife, a great revulsion set in, and the Green movement was born.

I give this thumbnail sketch from memory, as background to the present state of affairs, where some are passionately against making any use of anything unless it can be described as 'organic'. This is a word I do not perfectly understand, and an attitude which I do not entirely share, though I have some sympathy with it.

Whatever 'organic' may mean, and it is not the opposite of the chemically precise 'inorganic', it does not mean that you are to let nature take her course and allow insects to run riot without interference on your part. Lawrence D. Hills, whom I have mentioned before as the patron saint of the organic movement, was not in any way against slaughtering insects on a grand scale as long as you sprayed them with the right stuff. In a rather bizarre passage of his book, he tells you how to make a nicotine insecticide by boiling 1 pound of soft soap with 4 ounces of cigarette ends in 2 gallons of water, straining the mixture through an old pyjama sleeve and keeping it in bottles. I expect this would make a holocaust of insects if you could actually get around to brewing it, and the key is that nicotine qualifies as organic because it comes from a plant. The insecticides which we are offered nowadays are usually organic in the same way, being based either on pyrethrum, which is a flower, or derris, which is a root. I have no complaint about that, but merely note that they do not work particularly well.

Insecticides, though, are not the only problem nor are insects the whole story. There are several substances which are by no means organic that I either use or would use if I could get them. Unfortunately, some of the best of them vanish for no known reason, as happened to sodium chlorate. This very cheap and effective weedkiller was available when I started gardening and I kept using it until it was taken off the market in 2010. It was what they call a total weedkiller, which means that it kills everything, and it was very useful for killing the weeds on paths and such places as the gravel between the road and our garage. None of the merchants who used to stock it could tell me why it had been withdrawn, or why I could no longer be trusted with this substance which I had used for fifty years with no known ill effects.

I have heard it suggested that this was because the IRA sometimes used it for making bombs. It is true that if you mix sodium chlorate and sugar you get an explosive mixture, and if you also get some batteries and a flashbulb, and know what to do, you can make it go off bang, but nevertheless I do not believe this theory about the IRA. Sodium chlorate and sugar make a tricky mixture which is quite likely to blow up the bomber rather than the bombee, and the IRA have by now got much more sophisticated ways of causing explosions. It is my belief that the manufacturers withdrew it because it works and was cheap, and they wished me to use a weedkiller which costs more, as I am now obliged to do.

Then there was an admirable fungicide called, as far as I remember, Elvaron. This was just the thing to prevent grey mould on strawberries. This fungus attacks the plants when they are in flower, and a couple of sprays with Elvaron put a stop to it altogether. Then Elvaron disappeared, I know not why, and nothing has taken its place, so my strawberries have gone back to suffering from grey mould to a greater or lesser degree, depending on the weather. My sage advice upon this point is that if you find something that works really well, buy a good lot of it as it is likely to be withdrawn at any moment.

Fertilizers

The organic people greatly disapprove of any fertilizer that is not either compost or manure, or else is of any animal nature such as blood, fish and bonemeal. This gory combination was recommended by the people from whom I got my oleanders, but I disapprove of the fish element as netting fish and grinding them up to make a fertilizer which we can very well do without is not a planet-friendly way to behave. In general, I am with the organic people, but not exclusively so.

The great question is: Do organic vegetables taste better, or are they in some way better for us, than those fed with Growmore? (This being the obvious non-organic alternative for us gardeners to use.) My view is that it doesn't make the slightest difference. I have never seen anything to suggest that cabbages fed with nitrogen out of a bag would be in any way less nutritious than cabbages nourished with farmyard manure. As for taste, I believe this to be entirely a matter of freshness. If you grow beans in your garden and eat them within hours of picking them they will taste better than beans grown a hundred miles away which have been packaged and labelled in a factory and left to lie on the shelf of a supermarket. This tells you nothing. The true test would be to grow two rows of beans side by side, sown at the same time, picked at the same hour, cooked for the same number of minutes, and then set out in twelve dishes arranged at random with six from beans from one row and six from the other. I do not believe that the most sensitive palate could possibly pick out the six which had been fed with Growmore from those which had been fed with compost or manure. This is such an obvious test that I suspect it has probably been tried in secret, and the results hushed up, to preserve the momentum of the organic movement.

There is, however, a sound argument for organic methods, in that it is better for the soil. I read an alarming piece about the Green Revolution, which is the name given to an intensive method of growing corn in India. This requires heavy use of artificial fertilizers to produce enormous yields, and was said by the writer to bring about a slight loss of topsoil every year. As topsoil is of limited depth, and as it cannot be replaced, it was suggested that this method, which has saved many millions from famine, may eventually condemn further millions to starvation. Whether or not this theory is true, it is enough to convince me that I must treat the soil with respect and use manure and compost as the norm, and artificial fertilizers as the exception. I am well placed to do this, as we have three compost bins in the garden and a farmyard opposite with a friendly farmer who lets me have all the manure I want.

All the same, when my asparagus crowns came with the instruction 'Just prior to planting, apply a dressing of a well-balanced compound fertilizer', I thought it best to do as I was told, and the rose fertilizer that I put on the roses does not claim to be organic, so I suppose it isn't.

Seaweed

In order to regain some credit with the organic lobby I wish to say that I am a great believer in seaweed. I read that in times past the people of the Aran Islands, off the coast of Galway, used to grow corn by carting sand and seaweed to fill pockets in the rock. The island of Innishmore, which is the island I have visited, seemed to me to be largely made of rock, and if such an unpromising surface could be got to grow corn, I thought that seaweed must have most remarkable properties.

Then a friend of ours had trouble with his raspberries. Instead of being tall and healthy canes they were miserable stunted things, so he consulted a professional raspberry grower, who said 'trace elements!' It was a long time ago, and I forget what he put on his raspberries to supply them with trace elements, but it was a great success and his raspberry canes went back to being 6 feet tall. When something similar happened to our raspberries I thought 'trace elements!' but you cannot go into a shop and buy a bag of trace elements, so my second thought was 'seaweed!' As a piece of general knowledge I knew that seaweed was rich in trace elements, such as calcium and magnesium carbonate, so I put seaweed on the raspberries, since when they have been their proper healthy selves.

You can get seaweed in liquid form but this is an expensive way of applying it, and I use the powdered version. This is not very widely stocked, but you may be lucky and find some in a garden centre (there is a version made by the firm of Vitax) or you can get it by mail order. Now that I have discovered the merits of seaweed I use it regularly on soft fruit and roses, and sometimes sprinkle a little for luck on peas or beans.

Nettles

It is an old gardeners' device to make a liquid feed out of nettles. You get a sack or a net, put half a brick in it to make it sink, stuff it full of nettles and put it in a rainwater butt. I run a long thin wire through the top, to

hang over the edge of the butt so that I can haul it up when I think the time has come to take out the old nettles and put in some new – about once a month. Nettles are high in nitrogen, so it is particularly good for any cabbage-type plant that is looking pale, but I use it on almost anything that I feel would benefit from a tonic. I may say that it smells disgusting, so if you are in the habit of sitting near your rainwater butt, I should give nettles a miss.

Enemies and Strategies

Before I go on to the growing of vegetables and fruit I will discuss the gardener's enemies as it is as well to know as much as you can about the vulnerable points of the other side before you enter the field of battle.

The enemies of the gardener are very many, and I have occasionally thought that if someone were to start a movement called War on Wildlife, I might very well enlist. Leaving aside such inanimate pests as weeds and fungi, those with which I am in constant conflict are, in rough order of menace:

Squirrels
Rabbits
Birds
Slugs
Mice and rats

Caterpillars and insects

Wasps

To this list I might once have added deer and foxes, but by now I have got the upper hand of them. The deer, as I mentioned earlier, have not been a problem since we got a proper fence; foxes I have managed to keep at bay for several years by means which I will come to later.

Grey Squirrels

Those who see these creatures skipping about in the public parks may think that they are sweet and cuddly little fellows, which they most decidedly are not. They come at the top of my list because they would, if left to themselves, destroy the entire strawberry crop. Indeed, one year, they did exactly that before I got the measure of them. They do not just eat the ripe strawberries, they rip the green fruits off the plants and throw them around for their own amusement. In this they are like foxes which, when they get among chickens, do not just kill one and carry it off to eat, but slaughter the whole lot for the fun of it. If you find green strawberries scattered about, be assured that a squirrel has been enjoying itself at your expense.

They will do the same with raspberries if they get into a fruit cage, and one year, for good measure, they took to tearing the bark off trees in the garden. I could not think, at first, what was doing this. The damage was quite high up. I wondered whether a deer had got into the garden and savaged the trees while standing on its hind legs. The builder who looks after us took me aside and said, in an undertone, that he did not want to alarm my wife but he believed it to be the work of the black panther which was supposed to be at large and which he was sure he had seen. Then I noticed the same sort of damage in a wood belonging to a friend, and he told me it was the doing of squirrels.

You can either shoot them or trap them, and shooting them is best. An air rifle will do very well, but I am a poor shot so I use a .410 (pronounced 'four-ten'), which is the smallest shotgun there is. This is generally considered to be a boy's gun and beneath the dignity of a grown man, but it does very well for squirrel shooting, provided you live in a country area and have a gun licence.

Squirrel psychology is an interesting matter, as they are clever enough to solve the most intricate puzzles in order to get at food, and yet they are also extremely stupid. I once looked out of the bathroom window to see two squirrels eating corn meant for the birds, so I got my gun and shot one. The other ran off, but by the time I was dressed it was back, feeding beside the corpse of its dead friend, and got shot in its turn. You would think that if squirrels were as bright as they are supposed to be, they would have passed the word around by now that the Enfield garden is no place for a squirrel in daylight hours, but they keep on coming, year after year.

They have a weakness for peanuts, and you can use these to bait a walk-in trap which snaps shut behind them, but then you have the problem of a live squirrel in a cage. There was a report in the paper recently of a man who was prosecuted by the RSPCA and fined £1,500 for drowning a squirrel in a rainwater butt. According to the RSPCA, he should have taken it to the vet to be put down, which, they say, is the proper thing to do. Shortly after reading that I had to take our dog to the vet for an injection, so I asked him what he would do if I brought him a furious squirrel gnashing its teeth and snarling, and rushing from side to side and end to end of the trap, which is what they do. He said he could put on some gauntlets, get hold of it, and give it a lethal injection, but I think he would find that difficult. He did not show me the gauntlets, but I imagine them to be thick and clumsy things, whereas a squirrel is a quick and lively creature, so I should not be surprised if it gave him the slip, and then he would have a panicky squirrel jumping all over his surgery, upsetting things and breaking bottles. The alternative, he said, was a 'crush cage'. He might tip it into this, which had a device to squash the squirrel up against the side so that it could not move, then he could inject it. 'I should think,' he said 'that, on the whole, all that is rather more traumatic than drowning.'

'And what would you charge?' I asked.

'Nothing,' he said. 'We do not charge for wildlife.'

I can understand that up to a point. If someone brings in a damaged deer, provided it cannot be patched up and taken to a sanctuary, he puts it down. He does not charge because, if he did, people would stop bringing in such animals but would leave them to suffer. However, I should think that, on reflection, he might decline to be held to the idea that he was willing to put squirrels down free of charge. I presume that the RSPCA logic applies to rats as well as squirrels, and to mice as well as rats. If their idea caught on and the vet found that there was a steady flow into his surgery of people bringing vermin of one sort or another for him to put down, I expect he would get fed up and start charging something like £30 per head, which is the sort of sum vets do charge.

My conclusion, therefore, is that the best way to deal with squirrels is to shoot them.

Rabbits

At one time I had a little book called *Living with the Enemy* which was supposed to tell you what things rabbits will not eat, but it has got lost, the way books do. I do not think it was very much use, as in our garden they will eat anything. They are not supposed to eat lavender but they ate quantities of it; I would not expect them to like roses, but they gnawed them ferociously; you would think that holly would be safe, but they completely demolished a little holly bush.

From my observation, rabbits go in waves. One year there will be an enormous number, and the next year not nearly so many. The year they ate the lavender, roses and holly was a plague year, and in desperation I had most of the garden enclosed in a supposedly rabbit-proof fence of wire netting. This certainly checked the flow, but from time to time a rabbit would appear – indeed, still does appear – on the inside of the fence. My tactic then is to chase it, in the hope of finding the weak spot in the defences, which may be where a cow has put its foot through the wire, or else the bunny has somehow managed to burrow its way through. If I can't find out how it got in, I try to shoot it, and hope that none of its friends know of the secret entrance it has made to the garden.

A rabbit-proof fence is an expensive item. As an alternative I will pass on a tip from one of my neighbours who has satisfied himself that rabbits only eat young plants and leave established ones alone, so he puts wire netting round the small ones and takes it away when they are fully grown. His garden looks very colourful in summer, but I have to say that if a rogue rabbit gets into our garden it seems to chew things up indiscriminately; young or old, large or small.

Birds

In writing of birds as being among the enemy I do not, of course, mean all birds. I encourage birds. I feed sunflower seeds and peanuts to the general run of wild birds, and I like to see the hedge sparrows lining up on the top of the hedge outside the kitchen, waiting for their breakfast of mixed corn. Even those that I regard as hostile I do not hate in the way that I hate squirrels – indeed I like to hear the wood pigeons cooing and the blackbirds warbling; but the pigeons will eat the growing point of Brussels sprouts and the blackbirds devour strawberries with as much gusto as the squirrels, though they at least have the decency to wait until these are ripe. Nor do they confine themselves to strawberries, nor are blackbirds the only ones to eat soft fruit. Pretty well all soft fruit is vulnerable to birds, and furthermore they like to eat the first shoots of young peas, and also have a trick of throwing shallots and onion sets around apparently for the fun of it. To stop all this I use either netting or DVDs.

To start with the DVDs, these keep coming, quite unwanted, with the newspapers, and they make excellent bird scarers. Hung just above the Brussels sprouts they turn about in a breeze and flap about in a wind, and the pigeons do not like it a bit. Thanks to the newspapers, I never have pigeon trouble with sprouts.

For low-growing things the simplest course is to get some 3-millimetre-gauge wire, cut part of it into 5-foot-6-inch lengths with a wire cutter or hacksaw, bend these into hoops and push a few into the ground along the line of the plants. Then you drop netting over the top and weight down the ends and the edges here and there. Strawberries, peas and onion sets will all be safe like this.

I have raspberries in a fruit cage, but the redcurrants and blackcurrants, gooseberries and loganberries are outside, and these I just drape with netting when the fruit begins to ripen. This seems to be all that is necessary, but I have to check the netting regularly as from time to time some little bird gets itself tangled up by the neck or foot and has to be rescued, often by cutting it loose with scissors.

I will discuss the matter of a fruit cage when we get to raspberries, but will observe in passing that birds do not always stick to the established rules. I once came across a man who grew Brussels sprouts in his fruit cage and raspberries in the open, because the birds in his garden always ate the sprouts but never the raspberries. Also, because we live half a mile from the nearest postbox, for the past fifty years the letters we want to post we have left sticking out of the flap in the front door, and the postman carries them off. Suddenly a demented blue tit has taken to attacking them, tearing the envelopes and savaging the stamps. I think this is a pretty poor way of repaying my kindness in lavishing peanuts and sunflower seeds upon the blue tits, but I suppose that birds have no sense of gratitude or obligation.

Slugs

I cannot imagine why nature created slugs. Hedgehogs like to eat them, but otherwise they seem to serve no useful purpose, and will do a lot of damage if you let them. There are those who are nervous of using slug pellets in case the birds eat them, and where possible I use a net to protect the birds from the pellets rather than the crop from the birds. If I have some slug-attractive item such as a pot of lettuce seedlings or of basil, I raise it up on a couple of short sticks laid flat on the ground with the slug pellets under the pots so the slugs can get at them but the birds cannot.

Mice and Rats

Mice are the bigger nuisance because they eat a great many things, including potato sacks. They seem to like potato sacks better than anything, so most of these now have holes in them. They also like the potatoes, and the apples in store; they enjoy shredding bits of paper, and will gnaw unexpected things, such as an old shirt which got splashed with creosote. This had to be kept in the shed because it smelt too strong for the bedroom, and the mice ate it notwithstanding. I feel a bit bad about so doing, but I set traps for them, or else give them rat poison in a special bird-proof box with small holes for the rats and mice to go in, but which the birds are not supposed to use.

When it comes to crops, the worst thing mice do is eat peas, by which I mean they eat the seed when you sow it.

To put a stop to this I mix a little paraffin, say 2 ounces, in about a quart of water, and pour it along the row immediately after sowing. The mixture is not so strong as to affect the peas but the smell is enough to discourage the mice.

Rats are a different matter altogether. Your average rat is a cunning fellow. He comes by night to eat the chicken food or to scavenge in the compost, and Master Rat is too fly to eat poison when there is chicken food on offer. I thought I had found his Achilles heel when I discovered that he had a weakness for peanut butter, so I baited the walk-in trap with this and did indeed catch two rats in succession. After that the message must have got around among the rat community that peanut butter is dangerous stuff, because I caught no more, which shows that in this respect your rat is a lot smarter than your squirrel. I only see a rat very rarely, and I don't actually think that they do much harm.

I had anyway to give up trying to catch rats as I kept catching hedgehogs, or possibly the same hedgehog again and again,

as one hedgehog looks so much like another that it is difficult to be sure. Hedgehogs are very keen on peanut butter and do not seem to mind being caught in traps. A squirrel caught in a trap gnashes its yellow fangs, chatters and rattles the bars, but a hedgehog sits quietly waiting for me to let him out. When I open the trap he does nothing at all, but sits completely still, possibly in a state of euphoria brought on by peanut butter. Anyway, the hedgehog is safe in the knowledge that he and I are on the same side in the War on Wildlife as he is an enemy to slugs. To get him to vacate the trap I have to wedge it open and go away, leaving him to trundle off in his own time, possibly returning in the hope of a second helping of peanut butter on the following night.

Caterpillars and Insects

I have dealt with greenfly and thrips on roses, and the little black creatures on sweet peas. These pests apart, the main danger comes from caterpillars on brassicas and blackfly on broad beans. If you have a vegetable bed you will inevitably see the white cabbage butterfly at work, laying the foundation of a plague of caterpillars, and if you grow broad beans, then sooner or later the tops will be swarming with blackfly. You can squash the caterpillars if you are not squeamish, and you can pinch the tops off the broad beans, which is supposed to help but, in my experience, doesn't much. In either case I spray the plant with something which, according to the label, is safe to use but will kill insects. The sprays now available seem to me to reduce the numbers, but not eliminate them altogether.

Wasps

There are those who stick up for wasps, saying that they pollinate plants, like bees, and are therefore useful. I am prepared to live and let live up to a point. I don't like it when they nest under the roof tiles, which they have a way of doing, and I don't care to have a nest in a hole in the ground at the edge of the lawn, as has happened. We have a Victoria plum tree, and in the years when the fruit escapes the frost the wasps eat nine-tenths of the crop, leaving me the rest, and I just shrug my shoulders and settle for that. Then, in 2010, they attacked the raspberries in an unprecedented manner, and as a result of this I may have made a discovery which is greatly to the disadvantage of wasps and to the benefit of those who dislike being stung.

Before I reveal my secret, I must tell you that there are two main types of so-called wasp killer; the type that works and the type that doesn't. You have to read the small print carefully to see which is which, as they both come as white powder in plastic squeeze bottles labelled

'Wasp Killer'. If it contains pyrethrum, or something that sounds as if it might be pyrethrum, it is useless. If it contains sinister-sounding stuff called bendiocarb, that is the one you want. The effect of puffing bendiocarb into the entrance of a nest is miraculous. I think that wasps must work on a similar system to bees, and have a queen wasp on whom everything depends. From what I can see, worker wasps arrive at the nest, get this white powder on themselves and track it in to the queen, who samples it and immediately dies. When this happens, the whole lot die in sympathy almost at once. The speed with which this happens is astonishing. At one moment the wasps are buzzing busily in and out, then, within a couple of hours, an eerie silence has descended and the whole lot are, presumably, dead.

To get back to my raspberries, it must have been an unusual year for the wasps to hatch early enough to catch the raspberry crop, but they were devouring it all – not a

raspberry ripened but a wasp began to eat it. I looked all over the garden for signs of a nest but found nothing. Not wishing to give up without a fight, I opened a can of Guinness and divided the contents between two pots in which the wasps then drowned themselves fairly freely. After that, thinking the expenditure on Guinness might get to be more than the raspberry crop was worth, I switched to Fiery Ginger Beer and they drowned themselves in that just as cheerfully. Then I noticed that the supermarket was doing a cheap line in big bottles of lemonade, so I tried that, but by now the wasps had got expensive tastes and would not touch it, so I went back to giving them ginger beer.

I found that the best wasp trap was a 2-litre bottle of ginger beer about a quarter full, with the lid off. After a bit of exploring around, the wasps found their way in, but seemed never to find their way out. This was satisfactory as far as it went, but the snag was that the total effect was negligible, as there were still countless wasps busy eating the raspberries and ignoring the ginger beer.

Now comes the clever bit. I noticed that on their way to the ginger beer the wasps used to settle at one or two particular places as part of the exploratory process before they went into the bottle. 'Perhaps,' I thought, 'if I put wasp killer on those places, or puff some onto them while they are sitting there, they will buzz off home with it and present themselves to the queen.' So I tried it, and greatly to my astonishment and delight, it worked. That is to say, the next time I had a look at the fruit cage there were no wasps, and as they never came back, I assume that this simple subterfuge had done the trick. Not that I can guarantee it. I have only done it once, but if I ever get such a wasp problem again, I shall lure them with ginger beer and sprinkle them with wasp killer, and I recommend you to do the same.

William Cobbett and the Potato:
A Digression

That great man William Cobbett was, among other things, a forceful writer upon gardening topics. I will be quoting him in later chapters, and as his name is not as well known as it should be, and as he had particularly strong views about the potato, and as the potato is, in its way, by far the most interesting vegetable in the garden, I will say something about Cobbett first and about the potato later.

Cobbett lived from 1762 to 1835. It was the time of the American Revolution, the French Revolution, the Industrial Revolution; of the Napoleonic Wars and of the first Reform Act; of Pitt and Fox, Peel and Palmerston; of Nelson and Wellington; of Byron and Shelley, Wordsworth and Coleridge. This was the age in which Cobbett rose to be a successful publisher, an astonishingly prolific journalist, and an author much admired, either at the time or later, by such people as William Hazlitt, G. D. H. Cole, G. K. Chesterton, Richard Ingrams and, incidentally, me. He also, towards the end of his life, became a member of the first Reformed Parliament.

His record as a campaigning journalist is exemplary. Twice he made England too hot to hold him and had to escape to America. On his first visit he was acquitted on a charge of criminal libel, and later he was fined $5,000 for libelling a doctor. In England he was prosecuted three times. The first prosecution was for publishing a criminal libel, and for this he was fined £500; the second was for seditious libel, for which he was fined £1,000 and sentenced to two years in prison; the third was again on a charge of seditious libel, from which he escaped as the jury could not agree. He was a consistent goad in the side of authority and his difficulties and offences arose from such things as his attempts to have corrupt army officers court marshalled; publishing letters critical of the government's actions in Ireland; furiously protesting at the flogging of soldiers; and showing sympathy for starving agricultural workers after an outbreak of rick-burning. The charges of criminal or seditious libel were, at that time, devices to suppress criticism of the government.

Cobbett rose from lowly beginnings, which he was inclined to parade almost as an act of defiance of the class-conscious age in which he lived.

'My grandfather,' he wrote, 'was a day-labourer; and I have heard my father say, that he worked for one farmer from the day of his marriage to that of his death, upwards of forty years. The legacies he left were his scythe, his reap-hook and his flail. My father, when I was born, was a farmer. The reader will easily believe, from the poverty of his parents, that he had no very brilliant education; he was, however, learned for a man in his rank of life. When a little boy he drove plough for two pence a-day; and these his earnings were appropriated to the expenses of an evening school. What a village school-master could be expected to teach, he had learnt; and had, besides, considerably improved himself in several branches of the mathematics.

'A father like ours, it will be readily supposed, did not suffer us to eat the bread of idleness. I do not remember the time when I did not earn my living. My first occupation was driving the small birds from the turnip-seed, and the rooks from the peas. When I first trudged a-field, with my wooden bottle and my satchel swung over my shoulders, I was hardly able to climb the gates and stiles; and, at the close of the day, to reach home was a task of infinite difficulty.

'I have some faint recollection of going to school to an old woman who, I believe, did not succeed in learning me my letters. In the winter evenings my father learnt us all to read and write, and gave us a pretty tolerable knowledge of arithmetic. Grammar he did not perfectly understand himself, and therefore his endeavours to learn us that, necessarily failed.'

When he was twenty-one, Cobbett, 'like Don Quixote, sallied forth to seek adventures', and on a sudden whim took the coach to London. There, through the help of a business acquaintance of his father, he was taken on by an attorney 'who, happening to want an under-strapping quill-driver, did me the honour to take me into his service. No part of my life has been totally unattended with pleasure, except the eight or nine months I passed in Gray's Inn.' Unpleasant it may have been, but his time as a copy clerk served him well, as when, next, he joined the army as a private soldier, 'writing a fair hand procured me the honour of being copyist to Colonel Debeig, the commandant of the garrison. Being totally ignorant of the rules of grammar, I necessarily made many mistakes in copying, because no one can copy letter by letter, nor even word by word. The Colonel saw my deficiency and strongly recommended study. He enforced his advice with a sort of injunction, and with a promise of reward in case of success. I procured me a

Lowth's grammar, and applied myself to the study of it with unceasing assiduity.'

Cobbett's account of how he taught himself grammar is as remarkable as anything of his that I have read. 'I learned grammar when I was a private soldier on the pay of sixpence a day. The edge of my berth, or that of the guard-bed, was my seat to study in; my knapsack was my book-case; a bit of board, lying on my lap, was my writing table. I had no money to purchase candle or oil; in winter-time it was rarely that I could get any evening light but that of *the fire*, and only my *turn* even of that. I had to read and to write amidst the talking, laughing, singing, whistling and brawling of at least half a score of the most thoughtless of men, and that too in the hours of their freedom from all control.'

I have noticed, as a feature of life, that self-made men tend to know better than most people about most things, and Cobbett carried this to the point of knowing better than anyone about almost everything. I have sometimes thought that if you agreed heartily with him on any point he would feel obliged to change his opinion in order to prove you wrong. The few things about which he did not know best were those about which he declined to know anything. 'I never like to see machines,' he wrote, 'lest I be tempted to understand them. I constantly resisted all the natural desire which people had to explain them to me.

As in the case of the sun and the moon and the stars, I was quite satisfied with witnessing the effects.'

I trust that what I have written and quoted above will have persuaded you, if you were not already persuaded, that Cobbett was both a master of plain English and a most interesting man. Throughout his adventurous life he remained a lover of all aspects of country life – of farming and forestry, of dogs and horses, and above all of country people. It was this that led him to his detestation of what he called 'the ever damned potatoes'.

Cobbett's concern, if one may use so mild a word, was for the English rustic poor, from among whom he came, and for whom he felt so strongly.  English farm workers lived on bread, meat and beer, and he suspected a conspiracy by a lot of 'crawling vultures' or the likes of a 'great swaggering fellow in Sussex, that they call the EARL OF EGREMONT' to substitute the cheaper potato as a device to drive down wages and enrich the landlords, on the theory that if people live on cheaper food they can get by on lower pay. In 1832, when addressing a gathering in Newcastle, he told them that, 'For my own part, I have said before and I here repeat it in the presence of an audience on whose good opinion I set the highest possible value, that, rather than see the working people of England reduced to live upon potatoes, I would see them all hanged, be hanged myself, and be satisfied to have written on my grave "Here lie the remains of WILLIAM COBBETT who was hanged, because he would not hold his tongue without complaining while his labouring countrymen were reduced to live upon potatoes."'

When I said, in the first paragraph of this chapter, that the potato is, in its way, by far the most interesting vegetable in the garden, one aspect that I had in mind was that nothing else that you might grow could have inspired Cobbett with such passionate feelings. Furthermore I have in front of me an excellent book with the striking title of *The History and Social Influence of the Potato* by Redcliffe Salaman. This eminently readable book runs to 619 pages excluding the preface and index. It includes a bibliography of 25 pages which refers to some 25 books on each page, and so, as well as the monumental work itself, over 600 books must have been written which either deal with, or somehow touch upon, the potato.

You could not say as much for the pea, or the carrot, or anything else that you might grow.

Also, it is the only vegetable that you might cultivate which you could live upon to the exclusion of all else except for milk. If you lived on potatoes alone your teeth would be excellent, you would have plenty of energy, you would not get scurvy or beriberi, or the skin disease called pellagra. If you wanted to be perfectly healthy you would need to drink milk as a source of vitamin A for your eyes and of vitamin D to stop you getting rickets. 'The potato with milk in addition,' says Redcliffe Salaman, 'constitutes a complete if monotonous diet.'

I have never met anyone who lived on potatoes alone, but I once knew a man who lived for a time on nothing but sweet potatoes. There is, of course, no botanical connection between sweet and ordinary potatoes, but I think the sweet species must be pretty nourishing as well. The man I am thinking of was called Seichi Tada, and he was the Japanese manager of the office where I was working in Osaka. One day, in a spirit of idle curiosity, I said to him: 'Tell me, Tada-san, what did you do in the war?'

'Grew sweet potatoes,' he said.

'Grew sweet potatoes!' said I. 'How did that happen?'

'The emperor sent us to an island in Japanese Sea. He did not send any foods. So we grew sweet potatoes.'

'Was that all you had to eat?'

'Only sweet potatoes.'

Somehow I have a very vivid picture of Tada's war, with Tada-san one of a group of Japanese soldiers dumped on an island in the Sea of Japan, neglected by the emperor and uncomplainingly growing sweet potatoes. He seemed perfectly healthy when I knew him, but then I know a man aged ninety-one who spent three years working on the Burma railway, and his present flourishing state can hardly be ascribed to the healthy diet given by the Japanese to their prisoners of war.

In 1834 Cobbett visited Ireland, where his worst fears were confirmed and his loathing of the potato reached new heights. The Irish system was for land to be divided into smaller and smaller tenancies, parcelled out between landlords and sublandlords and between tenants and subtenants. At the time of Cobbett's visit there were about 700,000 holdings of less than 15 acres, and often enough these were further divided into mere patches of an acre or two, let at exorbitant rents. On these the tenants either rented or erected some sort of cabin, moved in and grew potatoes. The labour needed was not great, and a couple of acres would, it was said, feed a family of six on a daily diet of 7 or 8 pounds of potatoes each. The usual practice was to keep a pig which shared in the household potatoes and was sold off to help pay the rent. The only other source of income was from casual work on the landlord's farm, on wages as low as sixpence a day.

The Times of 1845 gave an example of the budget of a small tenant as follows:

	£	s	d
Wages	3	18	0
Value of pig	4	0	0
	7	**18**	0
Deduct rent	5	0	0
Balance	2	18	0

Only the potato stood between such a family and starvation.

Cobbett had seen plenty of rural poverty in England but what he met in Ireland sent him into a state of furious shock. As one of many examples, he describes a cabin of 10 or 12 feet square with a hole in the roof which 'in the cold weather the poor, ragged, half-naked creatures *stop up to keep in the smoke to keep them from perishing with the cold*!'

As to the contents of this cabin, 'there are, an *iron pot*, a *rough table*, or a *board laid across two piles of stones*, seats of stones, or a board laid from one stone to another; and that is all the stock of goods, except a *dish*, of which

I shall speak presently. The pig eats with the family, and generally sleeps in the same place. The potatoes are taken up and turned out into a great *dish*, which dish is a shallow basket made of oziers with the bark on. The family squat round this basket and take out the potatoes with their hands; the pig stands and is helped by someone, and sometimes he eats out of the pot. He goes in and out and about, like one of the family; the family sleep, huddled up together, on dead weeds or a little straw in one corner, and the pig, on a similar bed in another corner. The pig is the person of most consequence; he is sold to *pay the rent*: if he fail, the family are turned out into the naked air to perish, which has been the case in many thousands of instances.'

Cobbett died the year after his visit to Ireland. Much of the time that remained to him was given to fighting as hard as he could to prevent the conditions he had seen in Ireland from spreading to the rest of the United Kingdom. He did not live to see the great Irish famine which followed the blight of the potato crop in the middle of the century. The possibility of such a disaster, if not foreseen, had at least been postulated by Cobbett's close contemporary the Reverend Thomas Robert Malthus. 'Is it not possible,' he wrote, 'that one day the potato crop may fail?' As indeed it did when the fungus *Phytophthora infestans* first struck in 1845.

Malthus's theories on the subject of population are generally scoffed at, but as they seem to me to be perfectly sound and fully borne out by what happened in Ireland, I suppose I have not properly understood them. In his 'First Essay on the Principle of Population' he wrote this:

Must it not be acknowledged by an attentive examiner of the histories of mankind, that in every age and in every State in which man has existed, or does now exist,

That the increase of population is necessarily limited by the means of subsistence.

That population does invariably increase when the means of subsistence increase. And,

That the superior power of population is repressed, and the actual population kept equal to the means of subsistence by misery and vice.

Vice, in Malthus's terms, includes war, and misery includes famine and disease.

In Ireland the means of subsistence increased with the spread of the potato, and the population shot up in consequence, from about 5,000,000 in 1800 to 8,175,124 in 1841, according to the census for that year. Then misery struck in 1846 and in 1848, when the blight destroyed the potato crop. Within three years starvation and disease, along with emigration, had reduced the population of Ireland by 2,000,000. It eventually settled at about 4,000,000, being limited, I presume, by the reduced means of subsistence.

William Cobbett had a low opinion of Parson Malthus, as he called him, although they appear to have been on the same side in the matter of the potato, which they both saw as leading to lower wages and increased poverty. Anyway, it was the parson, not Cobbett, who foresaw the danger from a whole country relying on a single crop.

I occasionally tease my ultra Green organic friends by pointing out that the great potato famines were the result of organic farming methods, there being no other method available at the time. If the Irish had known how to spray the plants with a decidedly non-organic combination of copper sulphate and hydrated lime (known as Bordeaux mixture) or else with a similarly non-organic mixture of copper sulphate and washing soda (Burgundy mixture), the potatoes would not have rotted and the people would not have starved. My friends are pained when I point this out, and try to pin the blame on the Irish peasants who, they claim, wilfully persisted in growing a high-yielding variety of potato which was known to be susceptible to blight, rather than lower-yielding varieties which were resistant to it. This is unfair to the peasantry concerned. There was not, and is not, any variety that is immune to

Phytophthora infestans. It is true that the early potato varieties were less likely to suffer, because the blight tends to affect the plants towards the end of summer, but there was no way that this could be foreseen by the unfortunate Irish. Blight in this particular form was without precedent, unexpected and, for some years, unexplained.

Before I leave Cobbett, Malthus and the potato, I will add a personal note which, as it is of no relevance, may well be cut out when this book is in the hands of an editor. In looking at the *Dictionary of National Biography* I see that Parson Malthus, whose dates are 1766–1834, was educated at the Warrington Dissenting Academy before going on to Cambridge. Between 1770 and 1783 the tutor in *belles-lettres* and the *Rector Academiae* was my great-great-great-grandfather, Doctor William Enfield. I am pleased to know that the mind of the youthful Malthus was to some degree moulded by the instruction he received in *belles-lettres* from my ancestor. However, the duties of *Rector Academiae*, says the DNB, included 'oversight of student discipline, for which [Doctor Enfield] was entirely unsuited'. Malthus was said by one of his earlier masters to have liked 'fighting for fighting's sake', and I do hope this does not mean that my respected forebear got a lot of trouble and aggravation from naughty Bobby Malthus.

A Selection of Vegetables

'It is a most miserable taste to seek to poke away the kitchen-garden, in order to get it out of sight. If well managed, nothing is more beautiful than the kitchen-garden.'

William Cobbett

I f you buy some lettuce seeds and follow the instructions on the packet there is a strong possibility that lettuces will result. Many gardening writers must think that this is an original and interesting idea which you would not have thought of for yourself, as they laboriously give instructions which amount to saying, 'Do what it says on the packet.' I shall try to avoid this. If I start a sentence with such words as 'I sow peas...', please take it that I mean that I sow peas at the depth and spacing and in the general manner prescribed on the envelope in which they came. Anything I may have to say is to be taken as supplementary to, or possibly deviating from, those instructions.

I can only tell you about such fruit and vegetables as I grow myself. There would be no point in my trying to give you useful tips on growing beetroot when beetroot is something that I do not grow. I do not grow it for the sufficient reason that my wife doesn't like it. I myself do quite like it, but it would not be reasonable for me to bring beetroot in from the garden for her to boil, burning up a lot of fossil fuel in the process, just for me to eat it all alone. Similarly, if you should happen to notice that, among other omissions, I do not say anything about figs, this is because we have not got a fig tree, and we have no fig tree because I have never been sure where to plant such a thing, and therefore never got around to buying one.

Before we go further, let me particularly warn you against being in a hurry. I learnt this from a slow, loquacious Welsh farmer, about whom I have written in another book. If pressed to get a move on, his opening remark was always, 'You cannot hurry Nature.' Then he would pause, before adding, 'You have to wait for Nature.' Then he would go off into a soliloquy, on the lines of: 'When I was a young man, I was always in a hurry. Always wanting to do something. Always wanting to get on. I gave myself ulcers, I did – worrying. Wanting to get on.' Here he would pause again, before adding, 'Then I learnt. You have to wait for Nature. You cannot hurry Nature.' Having thus brought himself back to the point at which he started, he would refuse to budge.

I believe he was right. His theory certainly applies to the state of the ground, particularly if you want to do anything on heavy clay, when you have to wait for Nature to put the soil into a fit state to be worked. Beware of gardening correspondents who have a trick of telling you what you ought to do each weekend. You may wish to do what they say, but you may be prevented by the weather, or the state

of the ground, or the need to do something else. Do not fret. Keep calm, and a perfectly good opportunity to do whatever it is will, inevitably, turn up. You will never be fully up to date with everything because one never is, but if you wait for Nature you will not be far behind.

Rotation

Most of the vegetables that I grow come from a rectangular bed of about 12 yards across, east to west, by 16 long, north to south. It is fenced all round with wire netting to keep out the chickens, who live on the east side, and the rabbits, who may approach from any direction. It is divided into three roughly equal strips north to south so that I can rotate the crops in an orderly manner, which is what you do to avoid a build-up of pests and diseases. In any year I treat them like this:

Strip A – I manure this with farmyard manure and compost in autumn or early spring, then plant potatoes. When I have lifted the last potatoes I lime it, because next year it is to grow brassicas, such as sprouts and cauliflower, and lime is supposed to stop club root in brassicas. Once I have limed it I plant out leeks in some part of it, to eat during the winter. The leeks will all be gone by the time I want to sow or plant brassicas, which come next.

Strip B – is where the potatoes were last year. It is mainly for lettuce, Brussels sprouts, cauliflower, spinach, parsnips and carrots.

Strip C – where the potatoes were two years ago, is where the peas and beans grow, and the courgettes and shallots.

By this method everything gets manured, and likewise limed, once in three years. Our winter vegetables are leeks, Brussels sprouts, carrots and parsnips (though parsnips are a problem, to which I will come later). In early spring and late autumn there is spinach. From spring onwards there are cauliflowers, lettuces, broad, French and runner beans, and courgettes. I also grow shallots in preference to onions, and furthermore there are artichokes and asparagus in separate beds of their own. All this is not enough to keep us in everything all year round, but it helps.

Digging

The theory of digging has changed a great deal over the years. William Cobbett, whose book *The English Gardener* came out in 1829, insisted upon what he called 'trenching'. There is, he wrote, 'an operation absolutely indispensable to the making of a good garden; that is to say *trenching* to the depth of 2 feet at the least; and, as asparagus, and some other things, send their roots down to a much greater depth than 2 feet, the whole ought to be trenched to the depth of 3 feet, with a spit of digging at the bottom of each trench, which would move the ground to the depth of 3 feet 9 inches or thereabouts.'

It is all very well for Cobbett to say that this is indispensable, but I cannot believe that any gardener in his right mind would dig trenches 3 feet deep, then break up the bottom for a further 9 inches. If he did, I expect that in a couple of years, the ground would have gone back into the solid state in which he first found it.

I have never attempted anything so extreme, but when I first started I went in for a modified version which my uncle called 'digging two spits deep'. This is otherwise known as double digging, and sometimes called bastard trenching, and I think has now gone out of fashion. For double digging you make a trench about 10 inches deep and 15 inches wide, putting all the topsoil in a wheelbarrow. You break up the bottom with a fork, then you fill this trench with the topsoil from the next row of soil, and so make another trench. You keep working backwards like this until you get to the end of the bed, when you wheel the barrowload of topsoil round and tip it into the last trench. It is extremely laborious, and on our clay the benefits are purely temporary. I used to leave the topsoil in big rough lumps over the winter, and sure enough the frost made it nice and crumbly, so that I could break it all down to a pleasant smooth bed in spring. Then over the summer it baked hard and went back to its original state, so the whole thing had to be done again.

Then the firm of ICI came on the scene with a range of weedkillers which, they told us, would kill weeds but were inactivated as soon as they hit earth, and therefore did not damage the soil. The theory was, I think, that the topsoil having taken several hundred centuries to build up to its present state, there was really no need to disturb it. The worms would do all that was necessary by way of deep cultivation, and we had only to kill off the weeds with this ICI stuff and lightly scratch the surface to make a seed bed, or else we could plant things in the bare earth with a trowel. This is a tempting theory, and it can work pretty well, but I came to believe that digging has merit when part of the wall outside our house fell down.

This wall was built by my then neighbour, who fancied himself as a handyman but wasn't quite as handy as he thought he was. Nevertheless, the wall, which is about 2 feet high, stood up pretty well for some forty-odd years, but two years ago part of it collapsed and had to be rebuilt. Every year since it went up I have planted bedding dahlias along the outside. I feed the bed but never dig it. Then, when the wall fell down, the soil at the rebuilt end had to be dug out and put back, and in the following summer the dahlias in that part were much better than those in the part that had been left alone. There was a

clear and abrupt division, with good flourishing dahlias where the soil had been disturbed, and smaller, feebler dahlias where it hadn't. There being no other explanation, I concluded that it was the digging that had done it.

In the matter of digging the vegetable bed, the only digging I now do is to dig things out. It is here that the potatoes come into their own, as I plant them in holes made with the Driber and dig them out with a fork. The devilish clever result is that, as well as being manured and limed once every three years, the potato strip also gets dug over in the course of the harvesting process. There are some supplementary bits of digging here and there, such as in the lifting of leeks or parsnips and the removal of the stalks of Brussels sprouts, but any other cultivations are done with a hoe, or the mattock, and digging is otherwise a thing of the past.

Sowing

There are those who sow according to the moon rather than when the spirit moves them, and for this the rules are:

- At the start of the first quarter of the moon, sow below-ground crops.
- At the start of the second quarter, sow above-ground crops, and plant out seedlings.

The theory is that the waxing moon exerts some pull or influence upon plants. Do I believe in this? you may ask. If you judge by what I do, you will conclude that I believe it absolutely, because I follow the sowing rule strictly, and the planting-out rule if I happen to remember. Do I have any evidence that following these rules makes the slightest difference to anything? None whatever, but I follow them just the same.

In the matter of sowing there has been a fairly recent and entirely brilliant development in the shape of things called cell plug trays. I buy geraniums in the form of plug plants, and these come in things called cell plug trays. When you take the geraniums out you are left with a plastic tray of some 6½ inches by 7½ inches with a total of forty-two little cells, seven down the side and six across. These can be used for sowing any small seeds, and they are particularly brilliant for really tiny ones. Whatever it is that you sow in the plug tray, once they get going you thin them to one per cell, and when they look to be a suitable size for planting out, you push them out of the cell from below with the stub of a pencil. If you don't get any such trays by buying plug plants, you can buy cell plug trays in gardening shops. The ones I have seen look as if the cells are a little bigger than those I have described and this possibly is an advantage as the seedlings can stay longer in the trays – though I have never had any difficulty with the smaller version.

I will say for the benefit of any absolute beginner who may read these pages, when handling seedlings, you should always hold them by the leaves. If you hold them by the stem you are likely to squash them and then they die.

I will also pass on to you an idea which I got from Jeremy, the man who delivers the bottled gas on which my wife cooks. Having made a drill or furrow in which you are going to sow your seeds, says Jeremy, you should take a blowtorch and blast the bottom of the drill and the earth on either side. This, he says, will kill the weed seeds lurking in the soil, after which you sow your vegetable seeds and cover them with weed-free compost from a bag. The result should be that your seeds germinate and spring up with no weeds whatever to be seen along the row.

Now, I am not the sort of handyman who owns a blowtorch, but as I have a high opinion of Jeremy, who certainly knows a lot about gardening, I went and bought one of those flame-throwers with a gas cylinder which garden centres sell supposedly for killing weeds. I have to report that it seems to me to be entirely useless. They tell you to pass the flame lightly over a growing weed, which they claim will immediately die. This does not happen, or not in our garden, where the weeds take no notice whatever of being scorched in this way. I can pass

the flame over them and you would never know that anything has happened. As for giving bare soil the Jeremy treatment, it makes no difference at all, and I get just as many weeds as if I hadn't bothered.

This is a disappointment. I can see nothing wrong with the theory, except that it doesn't work. I can only think that perhaps a blowtorch gives out a more powerful and concentrated heat than a flame-thrower, and that possibly if you tried it with the former you would not get the unsatisfactory results that I have had with the latter.

The Cold Frame

Many seedlings, of flowers and vegetables, I start off in a cold frame which sits on the concrete slabs which form the top of the septic tank. The frame and the tank fit almost exactly, and they look as if they might have been made for each other. I hoped that I might have discovered some Green, low-technology method of heating a cold frame not just by the sun but also from the septic tank below. I thought that perhaps the bathwater and washing-up water would still be warm when they reached the tank, and furthermore that there would be some bacterial action which would generate heat, just as grass mowings heat up in a compost bin. Possibly there is some such heat, but, if so, it is not enough to warm the frame sufficiently to keep geranium cuttings alive all winter, because I tried it and they got frosted.

Artichokes

I grow artichokes in a bath. I speak here of the Jerusalem artichoke, of which you eat the knobby tuber, and of a bath in the garden, not in the house. There is no plumbing involved with the bath, it just sits under the hedge with artichokes growing in it. I grow them in a bath because a friend who gave me the original artichoke tubers warned me that they tend to spread. 'They will not spread,' I thought, 'if I grow them in a bath,' so I did, and it works very well.

I did not go out specially to get them a bath, but I happened to have one lying idle at the bottom of the chicken run. It is a plastic bath which another friend was going to throw away, and he gave it to me because I was thinking of getting some ducks, and an old bath, sunk in the ground, would do very well as a duck pond. Then I decided not to have ducks after all, so I had a spare bath available for growing artichokes.

I am, I admit, rather proud of it. There is a certain fashion for growing things in raised beds, and I do not see why you should not have a whole raised vegetable garden made of old baths laid out side by side, like beds in the ward of a hospital. This would be ideal for anyone too old and stiff to kneel or stoop, because you could raise the baths to any height you liked by mounting them on logs. I found that the legs of my bath began to buckle when I started filling it with earth, so I put a stout log under each end to support it. The log at the end that would be the tap end if there were any taps is slightly higher than the plug end, so that it drains nicely.

Under the bath I put a layer of black stuff to keep the weeds down, but if I were doing it again I would use roofing felt, as it would last longer. I filled the bath with a mixture of earth and compost and planted the artichokes about 3 inches deep in a double row, about 6 inches apart either way. Then they grew, and, indeed, flourished.

An artichoke is a kind of sunflower, so they grow pretty tall, but they do not seem to need staking, perhaps because they are sheltered by hedge. The bath is invisible from the main garden as the hedge hides it, but the plants can be seen above it. They are not exactly decorative, but they look quite pleasant. They are like hydrangeas, in that they hang their heads and look miserable if they are short of water, so then I give them 2 gallons from a watering can, whereupon they perk up.

They begin to go yellow as winter approaches, but you must let them die away completely before you cut the tops off to about 6 inches, otherwise, they say, the tubers stop growing too soon, and you get a smaller crop. After you've cut them down you can start to eat them. Frost does not seem to hurt them, so they stay in the bath and I fork some out from time to time for my wife to make soup. When we've eaten most of them, I lift the rest and replant them in a double row as before, and the whole process goes round again. They get a sprinkling of Growmore and a dressing of farmyard manure in the spring, which must help them along.

If you want to try growing them, either in the ground or in the bath, I suggest you buy the tubers from a greengrocer rather than a seed or plant merchant, as this will be cheaper. In the ground you should space them out more than I do in the bath – 12 inches between plants and

3 feet between rows are the recommended distances, or else you can try the Cobbett method, which is this:

> A handful of the bits of its roots, flung about a piece of ground of any sort, will keep bearing for ever in spite of grass and weeds; the difficulty being, not to get it to grow, but to get the ground free from it when once it has taken to growing. It is a very poor, insipid vegetable; but if you have a relish for it, pray keep it out of the garden, and dig up the corner of some field, or some worthless meadow, and throw some roots into it.

There is an altogether different type called the globe artichoke, which I have never grown and only eaten once. This was in a smart French restaurant in London, where they placed in front of me a strange-looking thing, being the head of the plant, all covered in prickles. I had no idea how I was supposed to eat it, and neither had my hosts, but one of the many advantages of being old is that you are not frightened of head waiters, so I called that functionary over and asked him what I was supposed to do. He explained that I should pull off the prickles one at a time and suck the minute amount of matter from the base of each one. After I had sucked the last prickle, I was to eat the soft centre with a teaspoon. It took a long time and was not at all sustaining, so I have never wished to eat another.

Asparagus

I can give you three opinions about asparagus, first Cobbett's: 'The asparagus is so excellent a plant, it is so good, and is so great a favourite, that it is one of the few garden plants that is worth the trouble and expense of a hot-bed.'

Second, L. D. Hills': 'Asparagus is too much fuss for a small garden.'

Third, mine: 'If you only have room for one vegetable, then grow asparagus.'

Whatever L. D. Hills may say, an established asparagus bed is very little fuss. Once it gets going it doesn't need much attention and it will keep you in a steady supply of the most delicious vegetable at a time of year when choice is limited – that is to say from mid April until early June. The only thing against it is that if you are asked out and given asparagus as a special treat, you have to conceal from your hosts the fact that you've been eating it almost daily for a month, and that the stuff they have bought from a shop is much inferior to the lovely fresh spears on which you have been feasting at home.

Having said which, I think asparagus may be a hit-or-miss affair. A friend, who is every bit as good a gardener as I, struggled with it for several years but only got a few spindly bits to eat, and eventually gave up. Ours, on the other hand, got going at once. It may be that it likes our clay better than his sandier soil, or it may be that I hit accidentally upon an important secret, which I will now reveal, as follows: to establish your asparagus, first grow a completely unsuccessful crop of sweet potatoes.

This, at any rate, is what I did. I was misled by some typically unscrupulous copywriters into thinking that sweet potatoes could be grown successfully in England. In my experience, they cannot. I sent off for the plants and set them out as directed in a bed 3 feet 6 inches wide by 18 feet long. They flourished like anything, and the whole bed soon was covered with a healthy mass of glossy green foliage. Then, in the autumn, when I came to dig them up, all I found was a lot of little red roots like abortive carrots, rather smaller than my little finger and quite useless for any purpose whatever. I dug the whole lot in and planted asparagus with complete success. I don't say that you must grow sweet potatoes as a green manure crop on the patch where your asparagus bed is to be, I only say that I did, and it worked.

It is best to get at least twenty asparagus crowns, or thirty if you have room. Ideally, for drainage, they should be in a slightly raised bed with well-rotted manure dug into it. You plant them 4 inches deep and 12 inches apart. Then you keep the bed weeded, and wait. In the first year you just let them grow, and they produce what is called fern, which in our case gets to be about 7 or 8 feet tall. This fern is apparently very attractive to flower arrangers, who must at all costs be stopped from cutting it – all the instructions insist upon this. Our garden gets a lot of strong south wind, and to help the ferns stay upright I put two stakes at each end of the bed, side by side, 18 inches apart. Then I join them all up with a length of plastic rope about 3 feet from the ground, running all round the bed.

The fern goes yellow in autumn, and then you cut it down to 3 inches and burn it. Each spring the bed gets a dressing of a compound fertilizer and a mulch of manure.

You are not allowed to eat any in the first year, but the excitement starts in the second. You take each spear when it is about 5 inches tall, and you cut it about 2 inches below the soil. For this it is a good idea to get a special asparagus knife with a curved, serrated blade. In this second year I recommend you to stop cutting after four weeks and let it grow. From the third year onwards you can keep eating for eight weeks, and you will find that it grows much like mushrooms. One afternoon you may see some tips just showing, and next morning they will be ready for cutting. The asparagus that the professional growers produce is always sold in slim, tidy bundles of a uniform size, but ours are not like that. Some look fairly professional, some are very thin, but lots are as thick as my thumb, wonderfully juicy and altogether delicious –

far better than those you can buy because you eat them fresh. If you want to save some for a day or two, perhaps to build up a supply for a lunch party, put the spears in a jug of water like flowers in a vase.

Beans

Among the various types of bean I grow the broad, the French and the runner. My favourite is the broad. One of my simple pleasures is to go into the supermarket in summer and see the huge dry-looking pods being sold by weight, of which the greater part must be in the pods themselves. The beans inside are bound to be as hard as nails, which I know because once, when my wife was out, I reduced some of ours to a hopeless mush by cooking them for twenty minutes. This was what it said in the cookery book, but my wife explained that the twenty minutes is for the supermarket sort, and for the fresh delicious things that come from our garden five minutes or less are all that are needed.

Not everyone likes broad beans, but if you find that you have some broad bean-lovers among your friends, you can gratify them with broad bean feasts such as they would not get in any restaurant, however well-heeled they might be. If I only grew one vegetable, and for some reason asparagus was ruled out, I would grow broad beans. I grow all three types of bean in double rows, each row with a strip of black stuff about 12 inches wide down the middle. By way of feed I scatter wood ash where they are to go, and give them bonemeal at the time of sowing or planting.

Broad beans stand frost very well, and will come through the winter from an October sowing. The old variety Aquadulce Claudia is said to be best, and I start them off in 5-inch pots, six to the pot, then plant them out 8 inches apart. In April and May I make further sowings 3 inches deep, straight in the ground, but at the same time I sow a few spares in a couple of pots in the cold frame, to plug any gaps that may appear. I favour dwarf varieties for these later sowings, but Aquadulce Claudia will do very well at any time.

There must be a framework of stakes at intervals along the rows, joined with string at about 1 foot and 2 feet from the ground, or possibly a little higher. Blackfly will attack them sooner or later, and all you can do is pinch off the tops and spray them with Derris or whatever else is recommended. I have not got the complete answer to the blackfly problem, but you need to have a sharp eye on the plants, and keep spraying them or the blackfly may kill them off altogether.

'Mice,' says Cobbett, 'are great enemies of beans, or more properly speaking, they *love them too much* as the cannibal said of his fellow creatures.' They may eat the seeds from the spring and summer sowings, so I give them the paraffin treatment as described earlier.

French beans I sow according to the seed packet. They are very prolific and do not need staking.

The best thing with runner beans is not to grow too many, and to pick them young. Eight plants yield quite enough for two, and twelve produce a surplus. I grow them up the same sort of apparatus that I have described for sweet peas earlier but without the pea netting, as they climb up bean sticks by themselves.

Brussels Sprouts

My aunt once employed a gardener called Jefferies who forbad her to grow cabbages and insisted that she grow Brussels sprouts. A cabbage, he said, will give you one dinner, but a sprout plant will give you many. She was guided by Jefferies in this matter, and so am I, so I never grow cabbages and always grow sprouts.

Cobbett has this description of the Brussels sprout:

This plant rises up with a very long stem, which has a spreading open head at the top, but which sends out from its sides great numbers of little cabbages, round and solid, each being of the bulk of a large walnut, and each being a perfect cabbage-head in itself. This little cabbage comes out just above the leaf which starts from the main stem, and it is in fact lodged in the socket of that leaf; and, as the leaves are numerous, there are frequently from thirty to fifty cabbages coming out of each stem. The large leaves are broken down in the month of August in order to give the little cabbages room to grow; and in November these begin to be in perfection, and continue to be an excellent vegetable all the winter.

In my early days I did not find that sprouts were round and solid, as described, but they had a way of opening out in a loose and leafy manner, nor were they a bit like walnuts. It said in the books that firm planting was the answer, so I stamped the ground around them as hard as I could, but it made no difference. The problem is now solved. The rotation that I follow means that the soil where the sprouts go has settled down and not been dug since the potatoes came out a year earlier, which seems to be what they like. I sow the seeds in plug trays and transplant the seedlings into holes made with the Driber, putting a pinch of Growmore in the bottom of each hole, and planting them as deep as the first pair of leaves. In our garden they have to be staked, and they need to be tied to the stake twice – once when they are young and again, near the top, when they are about 2 feet tall. I hang unwanted CDs between the stakes to keep the pigeons off.

Seed catalogues tell you that there are early, mid-season and late varieties. As they are not worth eating until they have been well frosted to bring out the flavour, I don't see the point of an early variety. I have sown some supposedly mid-season and some allegedly late ones in the same year and could not tell which was which in terms of when they were ready, so now I just sow one variety. Sprouts have this delightful habit of being ready to pick from the bottom up, so you work your way up the stem over time, and you can go on picking for weeks and weeks. They stand in the bed all winter and you gather them as you want them.

Carrots

I do not sow carrots before June, whatever the seed packet may say, because earlier sowings never seem to come to anything. Then in June I sow both Early Nantes and Chantenay Red Cored in separate rows. I grow the early ones as our grandchildren are either keen on juicy young carrots or else pretend to be in order to gratify their grandfather when they come to see us. In our heavy soil the stump-rooted later varieties are best, as they do not fork in the same way as the longer ones. I never thin them as hard as the books say. The late ones do all right at 2 inches apart, and I leave them in the ground in winter and dig them up in batches.

Carrot seed takes a long time to germinate and the seedlings are hard to tell from weed seedlings, for which reason Jeremy's blowtorch method has everything to be said for it if you can get it to work.

Cauliflower

I used to grow broccoli as a spring vegetable but I found that it all was ready at once, and had shot into flower before we had eaten half of it. I get on better with spring cauliflowers. Sow and plant as for Brussels sprouts, and if there is a very hard winter, hope for the best.

Courgettes

At the height of summer it becomes nearly impossible to give courgettes away, and it would almost be a kindness *not* to grow them, so that your neighbours had someone on whom to unload the vast surplus that there always seems to be.

My theory of courgettes is similar to my theory of strawberries, viz. that there is only a limited amount of flavour in each one, and the bigger they are the less they taste, because the flavour is spread more thinly. For this reason, as well as to control the glut, I keep picking them when they are not more than 4 inches long. All the same, there are always some which escape notice and turn into marrows, and these I chop up and give to the chickens.

Two, or at the most three, plants will produce enough for anyone, and the Enfield method of growing courgettes is this:

- In late April or early May select the places where you want them to grow.

- Sow two seeds on their sides close together at each place.

- Water them. Put a handful of slug bait on top. Put a big jam jar over the slug bait. Keep them watered, and wait.

If all goes well two little shoots will appear. I sow two in case only one germinates. If both sprout I pull one out and throw it away. If the weather gets very hot, I take the jam jars off, and if there are frosty nights, I put them back, with a bucket or clay pot over the top as well. As a reserve, I sow a couple more in pots in the cold frame.

My late sister-in-law had a rather crushing way with her, and liked to put me down if possible. One day I came in proudly carrying a bowl of delicious-looking baby courgettes, which she looked at coldly and said, 'Personally I prefer zucchini!'

'What nonsense!' I thought and so, in the hope of proving her wrong, I changed and grew zucchini in the following year. I have to say that I think she was right. I am not at all sure what the difference may be – indeed I suspect that a zucchini is just one among several varieties of courgette – but anyway it is the variety I now grow as they have a way of getting longer, rather than fatter, if you overlook them, and do not so easily become marrows.

Herbs

Herbs need to be near the kitchen, and so such as I grow are mostly in pots. There is a very big pot for mint, and 5-inch pots for parsley and basil. Slugs are very keen on basil, so the pots need to be raised up on some sort of frame – two sticks between two bricks would do – with

slug bait underneath. In addition there is a small bay tree growing at the edge of the lawn. Usually I grow chives but I need to get some fresh ones to replace those that unaccountably died.

I have had little success in growing either basil or parsley from seed, and so was pleased to find that a charity shop in the village has an enthusiastic supporter who gives them her surplus plants to sell, including little pots of basil and parsley. Such pots can also be bought in garden centres or even in supermarkets.

Lettuce

Spring after spring, summer after summer, I sow Little Gem. It grows well, it is a nice size, it is suitable for planting between Brussels sprouts. I sow Little Gem seeds in a pot, then use the Driber to plant them out when they are a couple of inches tall, and put a pinch of Growmore in each hole.

Leeks

Some years ago I was travelling on a train and fell into conversation with a coal miner. He began talking about gardening, and so I said to him, 'You fellows from the north are always keen on growing leeks. The trouble with my leeks is that half of them go to seed before I am ready to eat them. Have you any ideas about that?'

'You must never let them dry out,' said he. Since then I have followed his advice, and my leeks no longer go to seed.

I sow a line of the variety Musselburgh in April at some convenient spot, and water it well. After they sprout I keep them well watered until they are ready to be transplanted to where the potatoes were before. I plant them into holes made to the full depth of the Driber, i.e. 9 inches deep, and about 6 inches apart. I put a good pinch of bonemeal in the bottom of each hole, drop the plant in, and fill the hole with water. At least once a week, unless there has been a lot of rain, I fill the hole with water again. Earth gets washed in, the plants expand, and soon the holes have disappeared but I make sure that they do not dry out until the ground gets thoroughly wet in autumn. They do not suffer from any pests or diseases that I know of, and stay in the ground over the winter, to be dug up when wanted.

Parsnips

I like parsnips. I like them boiled, I like them roasted, they make excellent soup but they have defeated me. If I go into the supermarket, I get the opposite feeling from the one I get from looking at their broad beans. The supermarket always has a bin of neat little parsnips of just the size and shape that my wife likes. Those that come out of the ground at home can be the size of rugby footballs and not just forked but deformed, like mini octopuses.

It is no good my trying different varieties because they all behave in the same way. L. D. Hills says that manure makes them 'fork and grow coarse', but I don't give them manure and they fork anyway. Cobbett says that their cultivation should be 'precisely the same as for the carrot', so you look up carrots and he says the cultivation is the same as for the beet, so you look up beet and he says, 'There ought to be no clods, for clods turn aside the tap-root and spoil the shape of the beet. No fresh dung, by any means; for that causes side shoots to go out in search of it, and thereby makes the root forked instead of straight.' Well that is much the same as what L. D. Hills has to say, and doesn't help.

The seed packet says I should sow in February, but in the vain hope that it will keep them small I wait until April, which seems to make no difference. I wish I had asked my coal miner acquaintance if he knew as much about parsnips as he did about leeks, but it is too late. If someone would give me another spare bath I would fill it with sand and compost and see if that did the trick.

I do not like to be beaten by a mere parsnip, so I mean to have one last go, sowing the seeds in a plug tray and planting them out where carrots have been before. The carrots were neither forked nor swollen, so perhaps the parsnips won't be either. If that fails I will, to my wife's relief, give up.

Peas

I favour a variety called Delikata, grown in a double row with a strip of black stuff down the middle. The merit of Delikata is that you get two types of picking. You can treat them as a mangetout variety, when you eat them pods and all, and you can leave some to go on to be full-grown peas. I soak the seeds for a day or two in a little water and sow them as soon as they sprout, giving them the anti-mouse paraffin treatment at the same time.

I read a piece by a gardening writer who said she had difficulty in getting her peas to climb netting in the way that they are meant to adopt. Delikata has never given me that trouble. It grows to be about 3 feet tall, so I cut six sticks 4 feet long with a Y at the top of each, put one at each end and one in the middle of each row, and hang pea netting round the whole. Delikata goes up that without any difficulty.

Potatoes

William Cobbett wrote his gardening book before his visit to Ireland, and he allowed himself to take a milder view of the potato as long as it was only one among a variety of different vegetables.

'I am going to speak here of this vegetable,' he wrote, 'as a thing to be used merely in company with meat and not to be used as a *substitute for food*... It has been established by evidence taken before Committees of the House of Commons, that to raise potatoes for the purpose of being used instead of bread, is a thing mischievous to the nation. As a mere vegetable or sauce, as the country people call it, it does very well to qualify the effects of fat meat, or to assist in the swallowing of quantities of butter. There appears to be nothing unwholesome about it, and when the sort is good, it is preferred by many people to some other vegetables of the coarser kind; and though I never eat of it myself, finding so many other things far preferable to it, I think it right to give directions for the cultivation of the plant upon a scale suitable to a gentleman's garden.'

I am old enough to remember the wartime posters with the words:

'Eat less bread – more potatoes'

The point was, of course, that while England was self-sufficient in potatoes, much of our wheat had to be imported at a time when the U-boats were a menace to shipping. Bread was rationed, but potatoes never were. Whatever may have been said in the House of Commons,

I am afraid that Cobbett was wrong, and that potatoes are considerably more nourishing than bread. A diet of bread and milk would certainly be monotonous, as Redcliffe Salaman put it, but not, I think, complete.

Anyway, treating potatoes as something fit to be grown in a gentleman's garden, I now grow one variety only, what is known as a 'second early' called Wilja. I have grown the first early Arran Pilot, but it does not seem to be ready any earlier than Wilja, does not crop as heavily and certainly tastes no better, for Wilja is delicious. The only maincrop potatoes that I have grown were so riddled with slug and wireworm holes by the time I came to dig them up that I found the amount of waste disheartening.

I start Wilja sprouting, otherwise known as chitting, in egg trays in the garage under the window, and plant according to the phases of the moon. My method is to manure the ground heavily with compost and farmyard manure, make holes 12 inches apart, 9 inches deep in rows 30 inches apart. I put a good scoop of Growmore, say a dessertspoonful, in each hole, cover it with about an inch of soil, then put in the potato. After planting a row like this I use a hoe to draw enough soil over the top to fill the holes.

This method is deeply disapproved of by L. D. Hills, who says that using a dibber is a 'lazy way of potato planting' which can reduce the crop on clay soil by as much as a third. I don't believe it, but I thought that perhaps in a spirit of enquiry I should plant one row by his method and see if it made any difference. For this, you take out a 'furrow a full fork's depth', line it with manure or compost, cover this with a thin layer of soil, plant the potatoes and put back the soil. Then I decided this was too much trouble so I carried on as before.

Once the shoots appear I use the mattock to earth them up, which means covering them with soil from either side of the row. The purpose is to keep the frost off and to stop them going green. I keep earthing them up until they get so tall that they cannot be covered by this means any longer, and then I put slug bait along the rows and lawn mowings on top. I feel that using lawn mowings like this must be quite the wrong thing to do, as I have never heard of anyone else doing it, but it keeps the frost off and the ground warm and does no harm that I can detect.

It is not always easy to know when to start digging potatoes up. You can wait until they are in flower, but they may be ready before then, and it is worth scrabbling about with your fingers to see how they are getting on, and whether the time has come to start eating them. I dig them up when they are wanted until the end of June, and then lift the rest. I leave them on sacks in the sun to dry for a few hours, then put them inside the sacks and store them in the woodshed.

Last year many of those in store were frozen and spoiled, which is not a problem I had met before. Gardening writers like telling you about things they call 'frost-proof sheds', as if these were readily available and you could tell one when you saw it. Obviously any shed will give some protection against frost, but a shed of which the interior temperature will never fall below freezing is, in my view, a figment of their imaginations. If such things exist, our woodshed is not one of them. Last winter was exceptionally cold, and if I had studied Cobbett properly I would have been better prepared. He says the potatoes are best kept in a cellar, but 'if you can ascertain the degree of warmth just necessary to keep a baby from perishing from cold, you know precisely the precautions required to preserve a potato above-ground'. He does not tell you how to ascertain this degree of warmth – it cannot be done by experimenting with babies – but I accept that any baby would have perished if left in a sack in our woodshed last winter.

I have a solution in mind, which I have every hope of putting into practice before the cold weather returns. I mean to create a potato store which will be, in effect, a large thermos. I need something like a very big packing case, and the farmer over the road says he knows a man who regularly burns just the sort of thing I want. These are made of plywood, and he promises to rescue one from the burning and bring it along. When it arrives I shall put a deep layer of newspaper in the bottom, as newspaper is a good insulator, which is why tramps use it for bedclothes. Then I shall put some large cardboard boxes (like those that hold half a dozen bottles of wine, but without the inner dividers) all together as a sort of island in the middle. The space between the outside of the boxes and the inside of the packing case I shall fill either with newspaper or with wood shavings, of which you can get a big bale for £5 or £6. When the time comes I shall put into each cardboard box a sack with enough potatoes just to come to the top of the box. Over the whole I shall put sacks filled with newspaper or wood shavings, and as I think any baby could sleep comfortably in such circumstances, I don't see why the potatoes should not survive.

Shallots

Shallots, and onions if grown from sets, have a trick of seemingly jumping about. You press them into the ground in rows but they do not stay there, they get scattered around. I believe that birds are responsible. They must have some strange desire to pick them up and throw them about, and the easiest way to frustrate them is to put a net over the top.

My wife prefers shallots to onions and I think it is better to grow them from seed rather than the usual method of getting one old shallot bulb to turn into a cluster of new ones. I sow the seed in plug trays and thin to one per cell. When planted out they do not jump about and they grow to be big handsome shallots, such as might well do for the flower show if I polished them up, but I am not going in for all that again. When the top has withered you can tie them in bunches or hang them in nets in any airy place such as a garage, to keep over the winter.

Spinach

I grow only spinach beet, not the summer or winter varieties. This too I sow in a plug tray, not before August as there are plenty of other things to eat over the summer. When planted out it can be picked in late autumn, in early winter and again in spring until it bolts, when I dig it out and give it to the chickens.

Fruit:
Currants, Berries and Mrs Kelly's Birthday

ome long time ago I spent some fairly unprofitable
weeks at Birmingham University on a course on the
subject of Management. We seemed to be lectured by men
who had never managed anything, and every management
theory on which they lectured has been out of date for
years. Indeed, the most useful thing I discovered was that
management is subject to the whims of fashion in the
same way as women's clothes. Just like dress styles or
hem lengths, different management techniques come into
vogue, and go out of favour, with the passage of time and
for no detectable reason.

Among the now obsolete techniques that we considered
on this course was one called 'input–output theory'. This,
as the name implies, is the common-sense idea that you
should calculate the cost of what goes into an undertaking

and compare it with the value of what comes out. I have now, at last, discovered a use for input–output theory, by applying it to the growing of fruit as against the growing of vegetables. My conclusion is that fruit wins, partly on grounds of a more desirable output, and partly because of a less demanding input.

To lapse into plain English, most fruit is very little trouble to grow. Stuff that grows on trees will pretty well grow by itself, and stuff that grows on bushes needs very little attention. Strawberries take more work (or are more labour intensive, as we say in management circles), but they are the exception. The fact is that fruit is generally perennial, but vegetables are usually annual, so things like gooseberries give you more to eat for less labour than is the case with, for example, peas.

In terms of output, I cannot say that I get more excited by the first strawberries than by the first asparagus, but the clincher comes when you consider the matter of the deep freeze. Things that happen in the kitchen are generally (in management lingo) beyond my remit, but I am told that vegetable freezing can be tricky, involving activities such as blanching, and that the results can be disappointing. Soft fruit, on the other hand, you can just shove in the freezer more or less as it is, and it freezes very well. Strawberries are, once more, the exception, as they come out tasting of strawberry jam rather than proper strawberry, but frozen raspberries, redcurrants and blackcurrants will make it possible to serve a delicious summer pudding on Christmas Day to those strange people, usually of the younger generation, who do not like Christmas pudding.

The result, therefore, of the rigorous application of input–output theory is that, if short of either space or time, the best solution would be to have an asparagus bed and a fruit cage, and leave it at that, which is what I plan to do when I get too old to carry on as at present.

As things are now, fruit in our garden is supposed to be ready in the following order:

Rhubarb (which is not strictly a fruit, but never mind that)
Strawberries
Currants and gooseberries
Loganberries
Raspberries
Plums
Apples

There is some overlap in all this. The rhubarb should start in April and keep going through the main strawberry season, and likewise the plums should be ready while we are picking raspberries. Except for strawberries, rhubarb, and anything growing on trees, a fruit cage is a good idea, and in the case of raspberries, a virtual necessity.

The Fruit Cage

A fruit cage bought from one of the many people who advertise such things can be an expensive item, so I built one myself, and it collapsed. I did not feel too bad about this as the cage of a near neighbour also collapsed, and hers was not home-made but had been bought from a proper professional supplier.

In both cases the collapse was due to snow. I had used fairly thin metal poles to make the frame, and I suppose hers had something similar. Neither of us thought of taking the netting off the top at the end of summer, and when winter came the weight of snow caused the poles to

buckle. Having learnt from this, I am able to tell you how to make a fruit cage which will not collapse.

You need some stout wooden poles about 8 feet 6 inches long, and ideally 2 inches in diameter. You may have to hunt around to find a source, and possibly be obliged to settle for thicker poles, but they are not expensive and you do not need many. You could make a reasonable cage with four, or an ample one with six. Having got your poles, you need to borrow, or perhaps hire, a device called a post knocker. This is a very heavy metal tube, sealed at one end, with handles on each side. You need to have two people available, so as well as the post knocker you may need to borrow the services of a fit young man. You put the post in position, holding it by the middle; the young man lifts the post knocker and slides it down over the top of the pole, after which the first 2 feet or so of the post will be inside the knocker. He then lifts the knocker by a foot or more and lets go, whereupon it drops with a bang of the sealed end onto the top of the pole, and he keeps doing this until he has driven it about 2 feet into the ground. By this method you get poles much more firmly planted than if you were to try digging holes and hitting them with a sledgehammer.

Having fixed your poles, you knock a big staple halfway into the top of each one. Then you run a strong nylon cord through each staple, so that it goes right round the whole, after which you drive the staples right in. You now have a frame of wooden posts with a cord running round the top. You can use wire rather than cord, but I find cord easier to handle and it seems to last very well.

People advertise netting in garden magazines, and it would be wise to get their catalogue before you start, in order to see what widths of nettings are available, because this might influence the spacing of your poles. You need to buy enough fairly heavy plastic mesh to go round three of the four sides, leaving the fourth open, to be the entrance. This mesh rests on the ground and I fix the top to the nylon cord with twists of thin wire at intervals. You also need enough light netting to cover the whole of the top of the cage and then to reach down to the ground at the entrance.

Having used the plastic mesh to make a frame with three sides enclosed, you drape the netting over the top and down to the ground at the open end. If you fix the top netting in some permanent way, and if the cage does not collapse in winter, the netting may get torn by the weight of snow. For this reason I fix it to the nylon cord on one side with twists of wire, but otherwise with short bits of string. These I cut in autumn and roll the top back, to be draped along the one side where it is held by wire.

The netting that reaches the ground at the entrance I weight down with a couple of bricks. Now and again a sparrow gets in, so I roll up the net at the end and chase it out. Blackbirds, which are the serious menace, have never got in. The posts, the cord and the staples cost very little, but before you embark on such a project, better establish the price of netting.

Rhubarb

Rhubarb has the reputation of being indestructible. I have heard of a case where it was dug up and thrown away, an asphalt tennis court laid on top, but still some nice fresh shoots of rhubarb came breaking through. I can tell you that if you want to get rid of rhubarb, the stuff to use is compost made from the recycled garden waste which the council kindly collects.

One year, in a spirit of ecological correctness, I bought rather a lot of this compost, so I used it up by piling it high on top of the dormant rhubarb. As well as finishing the bags of compost I also finished off the rhubarb, which was never the same again. It did not die outright, but it produced thin, sickly stalks, so weak that they could not stand upright. I waited to see if it recovered next year, which it did not, so I dug it up and it gave up the ghost without any sort of resistance.

Otherwise it is pretty simple to grow, unless you try to follow L. D. Hills, who says you need to dig in 'a barrowload of wool shoddy – an old flock mattress will provide plenty'. Goodness knows where you could now get an old flock mattress, unless perhaps in an antique shop for a great deal of money. Failing such a mattress, you should dig in manure, or compost other than the recycled sort, where it is to go.

Plant the crowns 3 feet apart with the tips just covered; keep the bed weeded; if any flower stalks appear with a big lump at the end, cut them off at ground level. Do not eat any in the first year. In autumn clear away all the dead foliage and put on a layer of compost, and in spring, give a sprinkling of Growmore. When harvesting from the second year onwards, pull and twist the sticks rather than cutting them. You can go on doing this at least until mid June but then you should stop and let it rest. By this means I have got back to where I was before I poisoned the last lot of rhubarb with recycled compost.

Strawberries

My ambition, only twice achieved, is to pick a bowl of strawberries on 21 May, because that is the date of Mrs Kelly's birthday. Mrs Kelly was the founder and headmistress of the little private school to which my children went at the age of five. The custom grew up that on 21 May everyone should bring the headmistress a present, and so every child came clutching flowers or chocolate or something along those lines, as if the word had gone forth from Caesar Augusta Kelly that all the world should be taxed. One year my daughter arrived proudly carrying a bowl of strawberries straight from the garden, provoking cries of 'Look what Susie's brought!' This was impressive, though not, to my mind, as impressive as the quick thinking of her friend Amanda who arrived empty-handed having forgotten the occasion, but handed in a bunch of wallflowers which she had hastily picked from beside the path in the school front garden.

Much of the excitement has gone out of strawberries now that the shops have them all year round. Strawberries used to be treats to be indulged in in June and July, and they were always delicious. Now they are often pretty dull, and anyway I have a lingering feeling that to eat them out of season is immoral, especially if they have been flown in from foreign parts, a practice which is at once harmful to the planet and bad for the balance of payments.

Professional growers choose varieties which look good, travel and keep well, and they pump them up as big as they can by watering them freely. The matter of taste is subsidiary to these considerations, which is why they are often hard and generally disappointing. I have said of courgettes, and I believe it to be true of strawberries, that there is only a certain amount of taste in each one, and if you make them big by filling them with water you simply dilute the taste.

None of this applies in your garden. No nurseryman is going to sell you a dud variety and none of them will admit that anything they sell is anything other than delicious, so you have only to choose between those described as early, maincrop or late. I find that the best flavour comes from strawberries which have ripened in their own time without being forced, for which the maincrop or late varieties are best, as they get the longest and sunniest days. There are also some which are called perpetual or everbearing, or something similar, which are supposed to keep on fruiting from June to September. I have no experience of these, but I have ordered some which I mean to try.

The useful life of a strawberry plant is about three years. When any plant is finished it is best to replace it in a fresh part of the vegetable bed which has not had strawberries before, or not for some time. They should not go where potatoes have been within five years, as if they follow potatoes they may suffer from verticillium wilt.

I grow them in beds 40 inches wide, which is the width of a roll of black stuff. I have to do some digging for once, to clear the bed of weeds and to dig in farmyard manure and a little bonemeal. Then I cover it with black stuff, buried at each end and weighted here and there along the side with half bricks or broken tiles. The plants go in two rows 14 inches apart, with 18 inches between them, each one going into a small slit in the black stuff. Then I cover it with bark, and you need to keep the plants watered at first until they are established, but after that they should last for three or four years. There certainly used to be, and possibly still is, an idea that you should pull off all the flowers in the first year, and only let them form fruit from the second year on. I wonder whether anybody has ever done a trial to compare the total weight of fruit produced in the life of the plants if you do pick off the flowers in this way, as against what happens if you don't. I think you do best to take all the fruit you can get, including the first year's crop, which is generally quite good.

As well as picking the fruit, you have to net them, keep cutting off the runners with scissors, put slug bait on them just as they ripen, and watch out for ants. Ants, says Cobbett, are 'a very pretty subject for poets, but a most dismal one for gardeners; for it is one of the most mischievous of all things'. They work mischief on strawberries by nesting under the black stuff and possibly killing off whole plants, so you have to look out and give them ant powder as soon as you spot them.

If you can find a fungicide that is recommended for strawberries, then, subject to what it says on the label, you should spray them when they are first in flower, and again about ten days later. The fungus that causes grey mould attacks at flowering time, and you can do nothing about it after that.

In March I pull off any dead leaves with my fingers, just to tidy them up a bit. Flowers from next year's crop are formed in the fresh crowns in late summer, and to encourage them you should take a pair of shears and cut off all the old leaves after you have finished picking, but you must be careful not to cut the crowns themselves.

If you aspire to have strawberries on Mrs Kelly's birthday, you have to grow an early variety and cover it with some kind of cloche, either glass, plastic or polythene.

You can buy kits for this purpose, and I was told by a grower that the key date is 15 February. You gain nothing by putting the cloche on before then, he said, but every day after that is a day lost in terms of speeding them up. I have three separate beds, of the three different types, and cover the early ones.

Currants

I grow the black and the red, but not the white varieties. As well as being very keen on summer pudding, I think blackcurrant and apple crumble is actually better than blackberry and apple, though I like them both. Our two currant bushes are very little trouble, though they have to be netted against the birds as they are not in the fruit cage. I give them bonemeal and manure in autumn. Otherwise, I prune the black by cutting out altogether some of the mature wood from previous years, and the red by shortening the young shoots on old branches to about 6 inches. Sometimes caterpillars eat the leaves and have to be sprayed, but we have never failed to get all the currants we want.

Gooseberries

These too give very little trouble. I feed them in autumn, like the currants, cut out some of the old wood each year, and shorten any strong new growth by up to a half. They also may have to be sprayed to kill caterpillars, but that is all.

Loganberries

Our loganberry is actually a tayberry, which is a loganberry without thorns, and a most satisfactory item.

To plant a tayberry you need two long poles, like those for making a fruit cage, and these you knock into the ground with a post knocker about 3 yards apart, or more if you have space, up to 5 yards, as the shoots grow very long. You staple four wires from end to end, the first along the top, and the others parallel below at 1-foot intervals. Then you plant the tayberry in the middle.

Let us assume that this framework runs from north to south. The shoots which grow in the first year you train to the north, tying them to the wires and cutting out any unwanted shoots if there seem to be too many. The ones you keep will fruit in the second year.

In the second year you train fresh shoots to the south, and pick the fruit on the mature canes at the north. At the end of the season you cut down and burn all those at the north end, and you go on like that, with fruiting canes at one end, and fresh shoots at the other. Tayberries should be very ripe, practically black, before you pick them. They have a sharpish taste, and the blackbirds love them, so you need to drape a net over the whole, if they are not in a cage.

Raspberries

Raspberries and strawberries are the best of the soft fruit, and as this opinion is heartily endorsed by the birds, our raspberries are in the fruit cage. This cage is 6 feet 6 inches wide and 12 yards long, and along each inside edge of the long sides is a strip of black stuff 2 feet 6 inches wide – the special heavy duty black stuff called Mytex, though I should think that the ordinary kind would do if well covered with bark. The raspberries grow in the centre of the cage, between the two strips of black stuff, the idea being, of course, that I only have to weed the centre part, the weeds elsewhere being smothered.

There are two types of raspberry, the summer fruiting and the autumn fruiting, and originally I had twelve of each. In the first year all went well, and both gave plenty of fruit, but in the second year those of the summer variety all died. I could see no reason for this so I consulted a nearby professional grower.

'Ah,' he said philosophically, 'they do that. They are like sheep or chickens. They seem to be perfectly healthy one minute, and the next minute they die.'

Now I know this to be true of individual chickens, and I have heard it said of individual sheep, but they do not mysteriously die in whole flocks or whole herds, all at the same time. Raspberries, apparently, carry things to extremes and die all at once. He assured me that he had gone out one morning and found an entire plantation, which had been in perfect condition the night before, wilting and upon the point of death. 'It is best,' he said, 'to grow just the autumn sort as they do not seem to do it.'

He then explained that there are two ways of pruning the autumn variety. The usual is to cut all the old canes down to the ground in February, after which new canes will appear and fruit later in the year. The other way is to cut off some of the old canes at about knee height, and from these will come fresh shoots with fruit which will ripen earlier than the rest.

I have said 'some of the old canes' and for a reason which I now forget he said I should not prune them all like this, so I tried cutting some one way and some another, but found that the knee-high method did not work at all well, as most of the canes pruned like this just died. Now I prune them all to the ground, and I feed them with seaweed and manure in early spring. If someone puts on the market a fungicide suitable for raspberries I shall spray them twice at intervals when they are in flower, as they can suffer from botrytis and go mouldy.

Plums

Jonathan Swift, he who wrote *Gulliver's Travels*, when he felt the symptoms of senility coming on, remarked that he seemed to be 'dying from the top, like a tree'. Our fifty-year-old Victoria is also dying from the top, and every year I cut out a bit more dead wood, but, curiously enough, we seem to get more fruit from its few surviving branches than we did when it was in its prime. In those days the frost destroyed the fruitlets in three years out of four, and the wasps ate nearly all the fruit in the fourth. Possibly global warming has made a difference, because somehow it has escaped frosts in recent years, and given a small yield of delicious plums of which the wasps only eat about half.

All anyone wants to do with a plum tree is plant it and gather the fruit, the only other job being to prop up the branches if they seem likely to break under the weight of plums. Given the time again I shouldn't have a Victoria, but would get a damson called Merryweather. This can be relied on every year for a huge crop of damsons, big and sweet enough to eat raw, and excellent for jam and cooking. I think this is what my neighbour has, and he puts boxes of damsons by the road with a sign saying 'Help yourself'.

Apples

I have grown apples of several varieties, and reached the conclusion that the only one worth having is Bramley. It is, of course, a cooking apple, and it gets to be a big tree so you need to give it a lot of space. Apples can be grown on different rootstocks, to produce trees of different sizes, but Bramley evidently will not grow on a dwarf rootstock and so is always big. Our one magnificent Bramley takes a year off now and again and does not fruit, but otherwise, though totally neglected and neither pruned nor sprayed, keeps us in pretty good apples for about half the year.

I suppose it was, as usual, some persuasive copywriter who originally caused me to buy six different apples all on dwarf rootstocks. Their names were Cox, James Grieve, Orleans Reinette, Laxton's Fortune, Arthur Turner and Crawley Beauty. The first four were eating apples and useless. I do not think that it is worth trying to grow eating apples. From time to time some friend insists upon giving me what he says is a delicious apple from his garden, but it never approaches the glorious flavour of Cox's Orange Pippin, and Cox is such a difficult apple that it is best left to the professionals. Cox was a complete failure in our garden, producing small, shrivelled and scabby fruit, while the other three eating apples were not much better.

Arthur Turner is a large cooking apple which is good for baking but does not keep, but for Crawley Beauty I have a certain weakness. The name, for a start is almost an oxymoron, for it is indeed a handsome apple, and few things of beauty have come out of Crawley New Town. Then, it flowers very late, and so is likely to escape any frosts. It produces huge quantities of little fruitlets which have to be thinned in June, otherwise the ripe fruit is very small. If I wanted one apple on a dwarf stock I would have Crawley Beauty, but the most significant thing about my six was that they cluttered up the lawn and made mowing more difficult, so in the end I put them on the bonfire.

I have mentioned the need to thin Crawley Beauty, and this my sister said should be done 'with a tennis ball'.

'With a tennis ball?' said I.

'Yes,' she said. 'The gap between each fruit should be the width of a tennis ball.'

I do not know where she got this interesting idea, but I follow her guidance and if the Bramley shows signs of cropping too heavily, I thin the fruit on the accessible branches to be the width of a tennis ball apart.

The Pheasant Episode

From time to time we get a pheasant in the garden, and I am always pleased as I think it raises the social tone of the house by a degree or two. Peacocks are all very well, but noisy and a bit over the top. A handsome cock pheasant conveys a certain cachet as he struts about the lawn, which puts one way ahead of the Joneses without any vulgar ostentation.

One year a cock pheasant showed signs of moving in permanently, so naturally I took steps to feed him so that he would stay around. He quickly got the idea that he was on to a good thing and brought his hen friend along, and we would watch the pair of them wandering about the garden as if they owned it. Then the hen suddenly disappeared, until one day I came across her about 2 yards from the front door, right up against the wall of the house, nestling among the rock roses and looking rather nervous at the thought that I had spotted her. I tiptoed away and there she stayed. We would pass and re-pass a few feet from her nose; the postman and the newspaperman came and went; she never moved. A number of visitors came to look at her but she sat as firm as a rock and looked right back at them.

My pheasant-shooting neighbour explained to me that when she had hatched the eggs on which she was sitting she would take the chicks to a supposed place of safety, whereupon the magpies would eat them. 'I am not having that,' I said, and built a sort of aviary round her out of old wire shelving. She looked decidedly anxious, but stayed put.

In the course of time, eight eggs hatched. The chicks emerged from under the hen and rushed around like mice, falling in the water bowl or sitting in the chick crumbs I had provided. They learnt to fly surprisingly quickly and performed tiny aerobatics in the aviary. When I pushed some bean sticks in for perches, they sat on them at once. All in all, as pheasants go, they seemed quite intelligent. When they were six weeks old they were pronounced to be magpie-proof. I forget why, but just at that moment we had no chickens, so we had a large, fox-proof unoccupied area available for their use. Accordingly, we clipped their wings and moved them in. When their wings grew back they started to fly out, so my neighbour suggested I should make holes in the fence, known in the trade as pop-holes, so that they could pop back. They were not intelligent about the pop-holes, preferring to walk up and down the wrong part of the fence in a despairing manner, and I spent some time shooing them back to find the way in.

Still, it all settled down. They came and went. There were five cocks and three hens, plus the mother, and having got to this number in one season I began to wonder if, by arithmetical progression, I should be knee-deep in pheasants in the course of a very few years. Nature, though, took a hand.

One morning I went down and there was not a pheasant to be seen. There was no blood or feathers, so the fox had not got in. Perhaps some sly poacher had come in the night and collared the lot? I went to report this alarming development to my neighbour and from his garden I saw them, strung out like schoolgirls going to church in a crocodile, marching along behind their mother away from home.

'Never mind,' I thought, 'they will come back to feed,' but they did not. I used to meet them occasionally when I went for a walk, and sometimes saw them crossing the road, but they never returned. I thought it was a little casual the way they just cleared off like that, but I suppose they could hardly form up to say goodbye.

The original cock pheasant showed no interest in his family, never came near the aviary, and left the garden altogether. I am sorry about this, and should he ever change his mind and wish to start another family, the spot among the rock roses is vacant, and the mobile aviary can be spared from its current use as an occasional broody coop for a broody hen.

The Chickens

Our first chickens were survivors of a biology project. As part of our eldest daughter's A-level course she put some fertile hen's eggs into an incubator, then cracked one open every day and drew the embryos at different stages. The school gave her a few extra eggs in case some turned out to be infertile, but none were, so at the end she brought home half a dozen day-old chicks. These we carefully reared in cardboard boxes until they were big enough to go outside, and then I knocked up some sort of a coop and run, and have carried on from there.

It would be going too far to say that the eggs from our garden now have an international reputation, but I have exported some as far as Devon, in the car of someone who was going there on a visit and took them as a present. I say with some pride that when it comes to laying delicious eggs, our hens are generally considered to be in a class of their own. This I attribute to the conditions in which they live, which I believe ninety-nine hens out of a hundred would regard as enviable in the extreme.

They live in what is actually a pheasant pen. In the early days I let them be free-range to the point that they ranged freely over the neighbouring fields, so of course the fox began to take them. After that I kept them in a wire netting enclosure 3 feet 6 inches high, which the fox used to jump over at night and then tried to get into their house. Eventually I consulted a fencing expert.

'You need a pheasant pen,' said he.

'Then make me one,' said I, and so he did. Now they live in a little paddock about 30 yards by 22, enclosed by wire netting 6 feet high, with two strands of electric fence

running round the outside. The fox can neither climb over the top nor dig underneath, and several generations of hens have lived there in a state of safe tranquillity.

There is an ash tree and an oak tree just outside, and a weeping willow, a young tulip tree, two gorse bushes, a *Ribes* and a *Hebe* inside. Some branches of the oak sweep down to the ground inside and the hens often perch there on a hot day. Bluebells grow on a bank at one edge, and I have planted some wild daffodil bulbs here and there. These are spreading slowly, and I think that in a thousand years or so the whole will be a mass of daffodils in spring.

I cannot say with certainty that these embellishments contribute to the happiness of the hens or the flavour of the eggs, but it looks especially good in high summer. If the grass gets long I mow it, and then, with the trees in leaf and hens of different colours scratching around, in my eyes it somehow begins to take on the aspect of a poor man's deer park.

If you have enough room to indulge yourself in this way, then the colour of the birds is quite important. When we first had chickens my son also had some ornamental ducks. By this I do not mean the sort of plaster of Paris plaques of Peter-Scott-type ducks such as some people hang on the wall, but live ducks of an ornamental appearance with names like Carolina, Mandarin or Shoveler. They looked pretty, splashed in and out of their pond, and laid eggs which they were too stupid to hatch, and they were not, in any sense, useful. When my son left home and dispersed his collection I thought that the right chickens could be just as ornamental and would lay eggs into the bargain. Eight is a good number, as then you can have two white, two black, two red and two grey. Apart from looking pretty, this makes them easier to count. Eight red hens all milling about in a state of excitement are difficult to count, but if you are looking for two of each colour it is a simple matter to tell if any are missing. Black, white and red are easy to find; nice pearl grey are a little more difficult, but can be found with perseverance.

All such birds can be got as hybrid pullets, which is what I recommend, but there are those who like to get the more expensive pedigree varieties. If you go to a rare breeds show you will be tempted to buy lovely pure-bred pullets, and this is a temptation to which you can almost certainly succumb without any subsequent regret, as you will be proud to be the owner of such fine creatures. If you get Marans, which are black, they lay beautiful big dark brown eggs, and there is a small blue-grey breed called Araucanas which lay smallish blue eggs. The only snag with such birds is that they cost more than hybrids.

There are those who like to breed and hatch their own birds, but in my view there is everything to be said against it. For a start, you have to keep a cockerel, which is a beastly noisy thing and very likely vicious with it. I remember well the sight of my son retreating backwards out of the chicken run trying to fend off with a bean stick a big, white and furious cock that seemed determined to tear his eyes out. The hens do not require the company of such a creature to get them to lay eggs, and I cannot believe that they enjoy the statutory rape which will be inflicted on them over and over again. As soon as a hen feels that the cock has his eye upon her she runs away in terror, only to be hunted down, seized by the neck, and undoubtedly raped, as the question of consent does not arise.

Then you lose the services of a broody hen while she sits on her eggs and while she looks after the chicks. The chicks, when they first hatch, are certainly sweet and amusing, but they quickly grow into the scrawny equivalent of a human teenager, and Nature being what she is, probably three out of five will be cockerels. Experts can sort out the different sexes at birth but most of us can only tell the cocks from the hens when they are fully grown and begin to crow. Once they start crowing, they go in for crowing competitions. As dawn breaks, the first cock crows, which rouses the others to see if they can crow even louder, and between them they kick up a fearful din which puts an end to sleep altogether. Such sounds may be pleasant enough on an odd occasion when you are staying on a farm as a break from city life, but day in and day out, from sunrise to sunset, they get to be a bore.

What are you to do with these blessed cockerels if you do rear some? You can, of course, eat them. We did eat one of ours, but I think our palates must have been corrupted by years of eating the mild flesh of broiler birds, because the meat of our free-range home-bred cockerel was too strong and gamey for our taste, so I gave the others to the butcher. All of which would explain why I now buy point-of-lay pullets at eighteen weeks of age, and keep no cock to plague them.

Looking after them, once you have got them, is a simple matter. You have to house them, give them food and water, collect the eggs and keep their houses fairly clean. I have spoken of eight as a good number, but for eight you must have a good lot of ground. If you have too many birds on too small a patch they will scratch it up and make it all muddy and nasty. If you will settle for two or three, you can get a house with an upstairs and a downstairs, all enclosed, and handles at the end so that you can move the whole from one place to another. The birds then spend their days on the grass below and go up a ladder to bed, or to the nesting box when they feel the urge to lay an egg. With this arrangement you can keep them in the garden and move them around the lawn, even letting them out to scratch around from time to time if you think they won't damage your flower beds or get eaten by your dog.

We have two houses each with a ladder leading to the sleeping quarters. By ladder I mean a plank with struts across to give them a better foothold. When I get some new pullets I shut them into one of the houses by themselves for the first night, and open the door to let them out in the morning. As chickens are fairly stupid things, it takes them much of the first day to work out that they can now climb down into the open air, and the idea of climbing up again at dusk defeats them altogether. For the first two or three nights I have to go out with a torch and retrieve them out of the branches of the tulip tree or from under the gorse bushes, and put them on the perch in the house where they should be. In the end, they get the hang of it and manage by themselves.

For bedding they have wood shavings, which I buy in a big bale. The idea that birds do not foul their own nests has not got across to chickens, and so from time to time I put on rubber gloves, pick up all the droppings and scatter fresh shavings over the top. Chickens follow the sun, spending longer indoors in winter than in summer, so the houses need cleaning quite often in the dark days and hardly at all in high summer. The manure goes into the compost bin, but I have read somewhere that you can put it straight onto currant bushes with good effect.

I feed them layers pellets for sustenance plus mixed corn for a treat. The pellets go in feeders which I keep topped up so that they can eat as much as they like. Some people give them mash rather than pellets, but I found that they threw a lot of this around and wasted it. When I go to collect the eggs in the afternoon I toss a few handfuls of mixed corn around, at which they get very excited. Theirs is a tranquil life, and hunting for grains of corn in the grass is about all they get by way of mental stimulus, unless my wife lights a bonfire. They drink quite a lot in hot weather, and have to have water at all times, and the ice broken in water.

The size and quantity of eggs depend on the age of the birds and the length of the day. Pullets lay small eggs which gradually get bigger as the birds get older. All hens lay the most in summer, tailing off as autumn comes on, and, in the case of older birds, slowing right down in winter. Professionals fool them by keeping them indoors with artificial light, making it midsummer all year round. Much the same can be done by nurserymen who grow chrysanthemums, which can be got to flower at any time of year by adjusting the day length so that they may think it is spring when it is autumn or believe it is autumn when it is actually spring. This is all very well for chrysanthemums but I am not sure that it is kind in the case of chickens. Anyway, in my case it is impractical.

Most probably if you have enough birds to see you through the winter you will get a glut in summer, but it is always easy to find customers for proper free-range eggs. The best plan is to buy pullets in spring as they will gather sufficient momentum over the summer to keep them laying reasonably well throughout the first winter. It is difficult to know how long you should keep them. In terms of strict economy the proper answer is that you should dispose of them at the start of their second winter, because after that they cost more in food than they repay in eggs, but I let them go on for another year if they are laying at all reasonably. This is really because I shirk the idea of passing the death sentence on them when they are obviously full of pep and enjoying life. When it comes to the deed itself, I have to get someone else to kill them, not for sentimental reasons but because I have never mastered the trick of wringing their necks cleanly.

The difficulties you may meet are that they can die, get red mite, moult, go broody, or the fox may get them. There is not a lot you can do if one decides to die, which it may either do suddenly or by degrees. Sometimes you find one dead for no reason, either in the house or on the ground. More often they give notice that they mean to die by standing around in a miserable manner, possibly on one leg, with the head sunk between the shoulders, and then moving slowly and stiffly from place to place. There is nothing to be done about this except wait, because sometimes they recover, cheer up and become their normal chirpy selves, and sometimes they expire.

Red mite can be a nuisance. I have never seen a mite, but I am told that they are so called because they suck the bird's blood and go red as a result. The symptoms are that egg production falls off and there is a grey dust, like cigarette ash, in the house. There are then two things to be done. First clean the house out altogether and paint the inside with creosote. As creosote is very effective in killing the eggs of the mites as well as the mites themselves, the powers that be are tempted to act on the principle of if-it-works-withdraw-it, but so far, while they have not banned it altogether, they have contented themselves with making it difficult to get. Five-litre plastic containers of creosote substitute are easily available but the real stuff can only be bought in 25-litre drums. Why they think that creosote, which has been around for at least a century, should suddenly become dangerous, and why we cannot be allowed small quantities but can safely be trusted with large – these are mysteries, and naturally one suspects the dead hand of the European Union to be somehow involved. I can only say that I have heard, but am not sure, that the creosote substitute, as well as being harmless to us, is also harmless to red mite, so I bought a big drum of the dangerous variety and use that.

A second thing is to dust each bird with anti-red mite powder, which you get from a farm shop. Grasp both legs of the bird in one hand and let it hang head down for a moment. It may flap around for a little but will then generally keep still, when you sprinkle powder freely on its bottom and under its wings. When I buy new birds I creosote their house and give them this treatment as a routine, as I once bought some that brought red mite with them when they arrived. All of which sounds a bit of a carry-on, but do not be put off as none of it is difficult and anyway red mite is not too common and may never strike.

Moulting is something that happens in autumn or winter. They stop laying, shed their feathers, look shabby and awful, grow new feathers and start laying again. You can only wait, and as they do not all do it at once, the egg supply will not be cut off altogether.

A broody hen sits in the nesting box refusing to move and pecks you if you pick her up. If put on the ground she appears to be in a daze, from which she will gradually recover, probably then have something to eat and drink, and after that go back to the box. It helps again to have different coloured birds, as this makes it easier to spot a broody individual from the others which sit in the nesting box for the purpose of laying eggs. The cure is solitary confinement for four days in a broody coop, which is some sort of cage or crate with plenty of fresh air. I still have the aviary which we built round the hen pheasant, so a broody hen goes on the ground in that with water and corn to cheer her up. There should be some kind of shelter from the rain, which in our case is an old water butt that ponies used to drink from in the days when we had ponies.

As for the fox, in our case he is kept away by the electric fence, so I can leave the hens to go to bed by themselves and get up when they feel like it, but otherwise you have to shut them up at night or he will eat them. I once read of a nineteenth-century legal case in which a farmer sued a hunt for trespass. The hunt argued that they were in pursuit of vermin, and that to go on another man's land for this purpose is never regarded as trespass. The judge, however, found against them, on the grounds that he could not believe that ladies and gentleman went all the way down to Leicestershire merely to destroy vermin.

Vermin or not, the fox is no fool, and has worked out that towns are full of delightful people who express their love of foxes in many ways, such as by coming into the country to scream obscenities at children scampering after the hunt on their ponies. Accordingly Master Fox has moved into friendly territory to scavenge in their dustbins, eat their children's pets, and occasionally bite their children. It would be unkind of us country people to laugh, but we allow ourselves a quiet smile. After all, we did try to explain that foxes are not really very nice and do need to be controlled, but all we got by way of response was abuse and violence. Never mind all that. Failing an electric fence, you have to shut up your hens at night, most especially if you happen to be living the good life in Islington or Notting Hill.

Postscript

On 12 July 2010 we had a party. It was a garden party, which it had to be as there were about sixty guests and they would not have fitted in the house. The date was vitally important, as it was fifty years to the day since we first moved in, on 12 July 1960. The party was for neighbours, all of whom we had known for some time and some of whom we had known for fifty years, short of a day or two.

We had a lot of help. The friendly Irishman who runs The Cricketers public house lent us a tent in case it rained (which it didn't) or to provide shade if the sun blazed (which it did). Friends who had retired from the catering business came out of retirement and cooked food that was perfectly superb. My young friend Nick, who runs the village off-licence, gave us a generous deal on champagne and such things, all sale or return except for the ice.

The garden played its part well. The hedges were trim, the lawn was mown. The trees cast their shade. The lavender was in full flower and the roses in brilliant form. If anyone had wandered down to the vegetable bed they would have found it in pretty good order. There was room to stroll around, and space for our greyhound, who thought the party was given for her special benefit, to show off her remarkable paces before an admiring audience.

It seemed to me that the garden had chosen to peak at this appropriate moment. It had served the family well as a place for games and hiding Easter eggs and for sleeping in tents. Then, in recent years, I have had more time to give to it, and a bit of help with it, and it has become productive in all sorts of ways. I felt, and feel, very grateful to it, especially for putting on such a fine show for the party.

'The far greater part of persons who possess gardens, and who occasionally partake in the management of them, really know very little about them,' says Cobbett. By his standards, this is certainly true, and I for one do not pretend to the marvellous knowledge with which most gardening writers are blessed. Nevertheless, such things that I have discovered which might be useful to others, I have put in this book.

Sources

The works of William Cobbett which I have quoted are his *The English Gardener*, his *The Life and Adventures of Peter Porcupine* and his *Advice to Young Men*. I have also used extracts from the Irish dispatches which he published in his *Political Register*, and which are quoted in *Not by Bullets and Bayonets* by Molly Townsend (Sheed and Ward, 1983). His remark that he would rather see the working people hanged than reduced to live upon potatoes is to be found in Richard Ingrams's *The Life and Adventures of William Cobbett* (HarperCollins, 2005), a superb book which I cannot too highly recommend.

The full title of the L. D. Hills book is *Down to Earth Fruit and Vegetable Growing* by Lawrence D. Hills, first published by Faber & Faber in mcmlx (it says).

'The Pheasant Experience' first appeared, much as it is, as a contribution to a handsome book called *Liberty and Livelihood*, published by Travelman and the Countryside Alliance in 2003 (or mmiii if you prefer it like that).

OLD AGE

AND HOW TO SURVIVE IT

Edward Enfield

OLD AGE AND HOW TO SURVIVE IT

Edward Enfield

ISBN: 978-1-84024-776-3   £9.99   Hardback

'*Cicero remarked that old age is a strange business. No one wants to miss it, he said, and everyone complains about it when they get there. Not I, though.*'

Old age comes to us all, and Enfield wittily advises on how to survive its trickier obstacles, not least the people who suggest you must 'do something'. One of the great delights of the golden years is doing less – from DIY to dinner parties. In elegantly entertaining essays, Enfield describes how to enjoy the finer years.

'*he writes with a dry wit which had me laughing out loud*'
                                                    THE OXFORD TIMES

'*Enfield's writing is gently amusing*'
                                                    THE SUNDAY TELEGRAPH

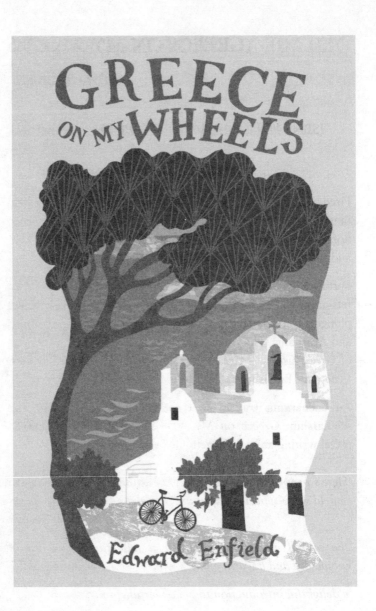

GREECE
ON MY WHEELS

Edward Enfield

GREECE ON MY WHEELS

Edward Enfield

ISBN: 978-1-84953-168-9 £8.99 Paperback

Fired by a long enthusiasm for all things Greek, Edward Enfield mounts his trusty Raleigh to follow in the footsteps of such notable travellers to Greece as Benjamin Disraeli, Edward Lear and the Romantic poet Lord Byron.

Fortified by delicious fish dinners and quantities of draught retsina, he tackles the formidable roads of the Peloponnese before plunging, on a later trip, into the rugged heartlands of Epirus and Acarnania. His travels are set against the great panorama of Greek history – Greeks and Romans, Turks and Albanians, Venetians, Englishmen and Germans all people his pages.

An enchanting travelogue that combines wit, charm and scholarship, *Greece on My Wheels* is a superb example of travel writing at its unforgettable best.

'Here's proof that it's never too late to hit the road – Edward Enfield's two-wheeled adventure is a delight from start to finish'
Sir Ranulph Fiennes

'the overall effect is charming... it will give you a bit of knowledge and a warm glow' WANDERLUST

'a delightful introduction to a wonderful country'
SAGA Magazine

DOWNHILL ALL THE WAY

Edward Enfield

ISBN: 978-1-84024-560-8

£7.99

Paperback

Fed up with questions about what he was going to do when he retired, Edward decided to get on his bicycle and ride from Le Havre to the Mediterranean. Armed with a tent and a smattering of French, he struggled in Normandy to get directions from old men tipsy on Calvados by 9 a.m., and hit his stride on the towpath of the Burgundy canal. He explored the mystery of what an *ouvrier* eats for lunch, and was barred from a swimming pool because his trunks were too decent. Through the Rhône and down to Provence and the Camargue, Enfield is witty and informative as always.

'*[Edward Enfield] is a terrific guide*'

THE DAILY TELEGRAPH

DAWDLING BY
THE DANUBE

Edward Enfield

ISBN: 978-1-84024-637-7

£7.99

Paperback

So Edward Enfield sets off on this enjoyable cycling trip, carrying few preconceptions but plenty of wit. Determining the route he should take from recommendations scrawled on a napkin, he starts by following the undulating 'Romantic Road' through the woods and cornfields of Bavaria – closely pursued by fellow countrymen in the form of a television camera crew.

After a solo jaunt around the rural backroads and Mazurian Lakes of Poland, stopping to enjoy the delights of Krakow, it's on to Austria, where he rides along the pleasant banks of the Danube from Passau to Vienna, taking in castles and baroque churches and sampling splendid wine en route. And, as Edward amply reveals in this charming book, there is no place from which to see a country that is nearly as good as the saddle of a bicycle.

'Enfield's stories will make you weep with laughter'
THE OLDIE

Have you enjoyed this book?
If so, why not write a review on your
favourite website?

Thanks very much for buying this
Summersdale book.

www.summersdale.com